paper books

Titles available in this series:

Lionel Abrahams
The Celibacy of Felix Greenspan

Michael Chapman and Tony Voss
Accents

Olive Schreiner
The Story of an African Farm

Olive Schreiner
The Woman's Rose

Olive Schreiner

The Woman's Rose

Stories and Allegories

Introduced and edited by Cherry Clayton

AD. DONKER / PUBLISHER

AD. DONKER (PTY) LTD
A subsidiary of Donker Holdings (Pty) Ltd
P O Box 41021
Craighall
2024

This selection first published 1986

ISBN 0 86852 073 X

Typeset by Triangle Typesetters (Pty) Ltd, Johannesburg
Printed and bound by Creda Press (Pty) Ltd,
Cape Town

Contents

Introduction

Most people think of Olive Schreiner as a one-book author. The book, of course, is *The Story of an African Farm*. Patronizing contemporaries like Cecil Rhodes were fond of telling her not to try to write another book, as it could not possibly be as good as her masterpiece. Rhodes himself had reason to be sorry that she did go on writing, and that her range as a novelist could embrace a satirical allegory like *Trooper Peter Halket of Mashonaland* as well as an evergreen existential colonial novel like *African Farm*.

Schreiner's range of talent and her versatility in handling different genres – pamphlet; allegory; satirical sketch; political speech; expository ideology; the broad sweep of history and geography in *Thoughts on South Africa*; lyricism and prophecy; descriptive realism; melodrama and pathos; short stories for children – have been obscured by the stereotype of the child prodigy and asthmatic governess who accidentally produced one novel of merit and historical interest.

The following short stories and allegories have been selected to provide a fuller and more varied picture of her achievement. Many of them still offer readability and charm, as well as insight into nineteenth-century feminism. They are also adjuncts to her longer works, offering brief statements of themes and situations which recur in the novels and non-fiction.

Schreiner saw allegory as an impassioned rhythmical utterance which blended thought and feeling, and all of her works have allegorical sections which she felt made up the core of the work. *African Farm* contains the best known of her allegories, the Hunter's quest for Truth. Her juvenile novel, *Undine*, also contains an allegory, and her posthumously published *From Man to Man* was, she said, an 'objective' version of the progress through the three heavens found in the allegory, 'The Sunlight Lay'. The feminist allegory 'Three Dreams in a Desert', included here, was once part of her longer study of women, which appeared in a truncated version as *Woman and Labour* in 1911.

Allegory offered Schreiner a traditional way of approach to abstract truth, a way of transcending individual lives and propounding what she saw as universal principles and ethical imperatives. Her allegories are both philosophical and moral, representing a valiant and ardent nineteenth-century struggle to achieve a new synthesis of belief in the face of crumbling religious dogma. This struggle stamps the allegories with their characteristic full-blooded and sometimes strained intensity. The issues were not peripheral. To the Victorians they were a matter of life and death. Herbert Spencer's *First Principles* was delivered to Schreiner by a miraculous stranger on a dark African night; it was a book which would offer her a free-thinking 'key' to the universal puzzle left in the wake of a receding Christian faith. Spencer, in turn, had Schreiner's Hunter allegory read to him on his deathbed. To Victorians like Spencer and Schreiner, only a morally strenuous but secular quest could replace the lost punishments and martyrdom of Christian, and especially Calvinist dogma.

Schreiner's allegories on 'the woman question' have to be seen in the same context. Readers approaching them in the self-fulfilling and liberated spirit of modern feminism may well find their moral intensity, and their emphasis on renunciation and martyrdom, both alien and alienating at first. Why was there so much to be given up, and so little to be claimed? Schreiner's female protagonists, like Dorothea Brooke in George Eliot's *Middlemarch*, if they enjoyed anything in a pagan, sensuous way, 'always looked forward to renouncing it'.

The detail of her mother's marriage that stuck in Schreiner's mind was the minister tearing a flower wreath out of the bride's hair, saying that such frivolities were not for a missionary's bride. Schreiner might have struggled to break away from her parents' religious faith, but the moral imperatives of selflessness and even sexlessness remained very strong. They cut across Schreiner's equally strong insistence on educational opportunity and the freedom to oppose conventional morality and conventional marriage. Modern feminism has been largely a sexual revolution. For the Victorians it was a spiritual and educational one. Allegory, as a genre, offered a fictional equivalent of Schreiner's own effort towards self-transcendence.

The repeated emphasis in these short works on renounced love, on men riding off into the sunset and leaving the heroine both free and lonely, derives partly from the ideological remnants of Christian purity and self-sacrifice. But it was also part of contemporary belief, influenced by a popular version of Darwinian evolution. What counted was not the individual but the race, and in this case the future of the whole female sex. Schreiner's amazingly popular book of allegories, *Dreams* (1890), enshrined a Victorian blend of mysticism and the secular creed of evolutionary progress. The 'dreamer' is the Darwinian prophet of race and sex: the individual had to be sacrificed to the progress of the species. 'Higher' beings, as Schreiner and her contemporaries somewhat complacently saw themselves, would be denied the fulfilment of marriage in the currently unsatisfactory state of transition, but those who came after would enjoy equal unions because of the struggles of their founding mothers. *Dreams* was dedicated 'To a small girl-child, who may yet live to grasp somewhat of that which for us is yet sight, not touch'. The wordy wistfulness of that dedication, though it reveals the Victorian woman who needed to carry her cross as well as give it up, should not obscure its fidelity to a historical truth. The battles of modern feminism have been fought over different issues, but only because more fundamental battles were fought by women like Schreiner.

Schreiner's separate allegories were almost all written during one particular period of her writing life, the mid-1880s, when she was travelling around Europe in some distress after the failure of close relationships in her London circle of friends. She had arrived in London in 1881, and the success of *African Farm*, as well as the excitement of London intellectual and literary life, had not brought her the personal happiness they might at first have seemed to offer. Her hunger for emotional intimacy had been partly satisfied by her close relationship with Havelock Ellis, but her need for a close and passionate relationship with a man had driven her toward mathematician Karl Pearson. Pearson's rejection of her, as well as the sexual competition which seethed below the surface of the 'progressive' and 'impersonal' discussions which were conducted at the London 'Men and Women's Club', had a searing and disillusioning effect on Schreiner. The love triangle which developed between Schreiner, Karl Pearson, and a married woman, Elisabeth Cobb (to whose daughter the collection of *Dreams* was dedicated), reinforced the painful lessons of sexual rivalry between women, and conflicted with

Schreiner's idealistic belief in female solidarity. 'In a Ruined Chapel', 'The Policy in Favour of Protection', and 'The Woman's Rose' deal more explicitly with this perennial conflict between emotional need and feminist principle. Schreiner's answer was, characteristically, an effort toward charity and forgiveness, and not the basic female competitiveness of 'Lord help the sister who comes between me and my man'. The focus on a love triangle might have stemmed from a personal crisis, but the conflict it explores is humanly familiar.

Dreams was enormously popular and well received when it first appeared. It was reprinted 20 times in England and sold 80 000 copies. Translations appeared in 8 countries. Schreiner's blending of solitary vision, didacticism, social concern and religious imagery spoke to the sensibility of the times. Arthur Symons, whose criticism introduced the English public to symbolist art, helped to create the high prestige of Schreiner's allegories by comparing them with the painted allegories of George Watts. Schreiner had seen Holman Hunt's painting of Christ, *Shadow of the Cross,* in 1886, and her own emphasis on martyrdom tied in with the pre-Raphaelite artists' focus on the figure of the scapegoat. Symons admired the otherworldly vision and prose poetry of Schreiner's allegories, praising them as 'pure symbols'. Schreiner's allegory, 'The Lost Joy', was published in Oscar Wilde's *Woman's World.*

The 'otherworldliness' of the allegories, their lack of a realistic social context, derived partly from the fact that Schreiner was travelling in Europe at the time, too restless and distressed to write longer works, and far from the familiar African terrain which provides a realistic anchoring for visionary flights in her longer fiction. This realistic context reappears in some of the short stories reproduced here.

Schreiner's short stories are perhaps more accessible to a modern audience than the allegories. 'Dream Life and Real Life' was written before her departure from Africa in 1881. It has many parallels with *African Farm,* dealing with the oppression of children, interweaving allegory and realism, historical authenticity and fantasy. Like 'The Wax Doll and the Stepmother', it has a child protagonist and was perhaps partly intended for a young audience. Schreiner's story-telling habits had grown up in the context of teaching young children as a governess in the Cradock area, and she had always enjoyed telling stories to children. Some of her stories for children were first published in her brother Fred's school journal, the *New College Magazine*, when Schreiner arrived in England.

'The Buddhist Priest's Wife', which Schreiner considered her most complete statement on the position of women, is clearly close to autobiography, but it dramatizes and discusses many of the issues of Victorian feminism. So does 'The Policy in Favour of Protection'. London is usually the setting of Schreiner's socialist and overtly feminist stories. 'Eighteen Ninety-nine' demonstrates the fusion of emotional participation and narrative skill which seems to occur when Schreiner's writing is in close relation to African realities. Written in 1904, it was one of a group of stories Schreiner planned to write, all to be based on incidents from the Anglo-Boer War. Originally titled 'The Last of the Van der Spuys' and then 'Elandslaagte', it demonstrates what Schreiner could do with the short story form when her sympathies were deeply engaged by contemporary South African issues. The elegiac mood of the story and the vigorous simplicity of its style make it a moving record of a phase of South African history.

The stories and allegories that follow have been arranged to show some of the interweavings of Schreiner's thoughts and feelings about women. They give us an insight into the central emphases of Victorian feminism. They reveal the characteristic morally earnest colouring of Schreiner's sensibility, an intense response to oppression, and to African landscape. Schreiner is of interest to the modern reader both as an example of historical conditioning and for her attempt to peer over the shoulders of her contemporaries into the future. The psychological and moral realities which she dramatizes have not really changed, and Schreiner's own lifelong struggle to keep the impulses of charity and sisterhood alive remains morally admirable and rare. 'It's hatred that grows like a fungus over human life' she once wrote. These short allegories and stories testify to her efforts to keep larger sympathies alive and pass them on in the form of fiction.

I Dream Life and Real Life

A Little African Story

Little Jannita sat alone beside a milkbush. Before her and behind her stretched the plain, covered with red sand and thorny Karroo bushes; and here and there a milkbush, looking like a bundle of pale green rods tied together. Not a tree was to be seen anywhere, except on the banks of the river, and that was far away, and the sun beat on her head. Round her fed the angora goats she was herding; pretty things, especially the little ones, with white silky curls that touched the ground. But Jannita sat crying. If an angel should gather up in his cup all the tears that have been shed, I think the bitterest would be those of children.

By and by she was so tired, and the sun was so hot, she laid her head against the milkbush, and dropped asleep.

She dreamed a beautiful dream. She thought that when she went back to the farmhouse in the evening, the walls were covered with vines and roses, and the kraals were not made of red stone, but of lilac-trees full of blossom. And the fat old Boer smiled at her, and the stick he held across the door for the goats to jump over was a lily rod with seven blossoms at the end. When she went to the house her mistress gave her a whole roosterkoek for her supper, and the mistress's daughter had stuck a rose in the cake; and her mistress's son-in-law said 'Thank you!' when she pulled off his boots, and did not kick her.

It was a beautiful dream.

While she lay thus dreaming, one of the little kids came and licked her on her cheek, because of the salt from her dried-up tears. And in her dream she was not a poor indentured child any more, living with Boers. It was her father who kissed her. He said he had only been asleep – that day when he lay down under the thorn-bush; he had not really died. He felt her hair, and said it was grown long and silky, and he said they would go back to Denmark now. He asked her why her feet were bare, and what the marks on her back were. Then he put her head on his shoulder, and picked her up, and carried her away, away! She laughed – she could feel her face against his brown beard. His arms were so strong.

As she lay there dreaming with the ants running over her naked feet, and with her brown curls lying in the sand, a Hottentot came up to her. He was dressed in ragged yellow trousers, and a dirty shirt, and torn jacket. He had a red handkerchief round his head, and a felt hat above that. His nose was flat, his eyes like slits, and the wool on his head was gathered into little round balls. He came to the milkbush, and looked at the little girl lying in the hot sun. Then he walked off, and caught one of the fattest little angora goats, and held its mouth fast, as he stuck it under his arm. He looked back to see that she was still sleeping, and jumped down into one of the sloots. He walked down the bed of the sloot a little way and came to an overhanging bank, under which, sitting on the red sand, were two men. One was a tiny, ragged old Bushman, four feet high; the other was an English navvy in a dark blue blouse. They cut the kid's throat with the navvy's long knife, and covered up the blood with sand, and buried the entrails and skin. Then they talked, and quarrelled a little; and then they talked quietly again.

The Hottentot man put a leg of the kid under his coat and left the rest of the meat for the two in the sloot and walked away.

When little Jannita awoke it was almost sunset. She sat up very frightened, but her goats were all about her. She began to drive them home. 'I do not think there are any lost,' she said.

Dirk, the Hottentot, had brought his flock home already, and stood at the kraal door with his ragged yellow trousers. The fat old Boer put his stick across the door, and let Jannita's goats jump over, one by one. He counted them. When the last jumped over: 'Have you been to sleep today?' he said; 'there is one missing.'

Then little Jannita knew what was coming, and she said, in a low voice, 'No.' And then she felt in her heart that deadly sickness that you feel when you tell a lie; and again she said, 'Yes.'

'Do you think you will have any supper this evening?' said the Boer.

'No,' said Jannita.

'What do you think you will have?'

'I don't know,' said Jannita.

'Give me your whip,' said the Boer to Dirk, the Hottentot.

The moon was all but full that night. Oh, but its light was beautiful!

The little girl crept to the door of the outhouse where she slept, and looked at it. When you are hungry, and very, very sore, you do not cry. She leaned her chin on one hand, and looked, with her great dove's eyes – the other hand was cut open, so she wrapped it in her pinafore. She looked across the plain at the sand and the low Karroo bushes, with the moonlight on them.

Presently, there came slowly, from far away, a wild springbuck. It came close to the house, and stood looking at it in wonder, while the moonlight glinted on its horns, and in its great eyes. It stood wondering at the red brick walls, and the girl watched it. Then, suddenly, as if it scorned it all, it curved its beautiful back and turned; and away it fled over the bushes and sand, like a sheeny streak of white lightning. She stood up to watch it. So free, so free! Away, away! She watched, till she could see it no more on the wide plain.

Her heart swelled, larger, larger, larger: she uttered a low cry; and without waiting, pausing, thinking, she followed on its track. Away, away, away! 'I – I also!' she said, 'I – I also!'

When at last her legs began to tremble under her, and she stopped to breathe, the house was a speck behind her. She dropped on the earth, and held her panting sides.

She began to think now.

If she stayed on the plain they would trace her footsteps in the morning and catch her; but if she waded in the water in the bed of the river they would not be able to find her footmarks; and she would hide, there where the rocks and the koppies were.

So she stood up and walked towards the river. The water in the river was low; just a line of silver in the broad bed of sand, here and there broadening into a pool. She stepped into it, and bathed her feet in the delicious cold water. Up and up the stream she walked, where it rattled over the pebbles, and past where the farmhouse lay; and where the rocks were large, she leaped from one to the other. The night wind in her face made her strong – she laughed. She had never felt such night wind before. So the night smells to the wild bucks, because they are free! A free thing feels as a chained thing never can.

At last she came to a place where the willows grew on each side of the river, and trailed their long branches on the sandy bed. She could not tell why, she could not tell the reason, but a feeling of fear came over her.

On the left bank rose a chain of koppies and a precipice of rocks. Between the precipice and the river bank there was a narrow path covered by the fragments of fallen rock. And upon the summit of the precipice a kiepersol tree grew, whose palm-like leaves were clearly cut out against the night sky. The rocks cast a deep shadow, and the willow trees, on either side of the river. She paused, looked up and about her, and then ran on, fearful.

'What was I afraid of? How foolish I have been!' she said, when she came to a place where the trees were not so close together. And she stood still and looked back and shivered.

At last her steps grew wearier and wearier. She was very sleepy now, she could scarcely lift her feet. She stepped out of the river-bed. She only saw that the rocks about her were wild, as though many little koppies had been broken up and strewn upon the ground, lay down at the foot of an aloe, and fell asleep.

But, in the morning, she saw what a glorious place it was. The rocks were piled on one another, and tossed this way and that. Prickly pears grew among them, and there were no less than six kiepersol trees scattered here and there among the broken koppies. In the rocks there were hundreds of homes for the coneys, and from the crevices wild asparagus hung down. She ran to the river, bathed in the clear cold water, and tossed it over her head. She sang aloud. All the songs she knew were sad, so she could not sing them now, she was glad, she was so free; but she sang the notes without the words, as the kokkewiets do. Singing and jumping all the way, she went back, and took a sharp stone, and cut at the root of a kiepersol, and got out a large piece, as long as her arm, and sat to chew it. Two coneys came out on the rock above her head and peeped at her. She held them out a piece, but they did not want it, and ran away.

It was very delicious to her. Kiepersol is like raw quince, when it is very green; but she liked it. When good food is thrown at you by other people, strange to say, it is very bitter; but whatever you find yourself is sweet!

When she had finished she dug out another piece, and went to look for a pantry to put it in. At the top of a heap of rocks up which she clambered she found that some large stones stood apart but met at the top, making a room.

'Oh, this is my little home!' she said.

At the top and all round it was closed, only in the front it was open. There was a beautiful shelf in the wall for the kiepersol, and she scrambled down again. She brought a great branch of prickly pear, and stuck it in a crevice before the door, and hung wild asparagus over it, till it looked as though it grew there. No one could see that there was a room there, for she left only a tiny opening, and hung a branch of feathery asparagus over it. Then she crept in to see how it looked. There was a glorious soft green light. Then she went out and picked some of those purple little ground flowers – you know them – those that keep their faces close to the ground, but when you turn them up and look at them they are deep blue eyes looking into yours! She took them with a little earth, and put them in the crevices between the rocks; and so the room was quite furnished. Afterwards she went down to the river and brought her arms full of willow, and made a lovely bed; and, because the weather was very hot, she lay down to rest upon it.

She went to sleep soon, and slept long, for she was very weak. Late in the afternoon she was awakened by a few cold drops falling on her face. She sat up. A great and fierce thunderstorm had been raging, and a few of the cool drops had fallen through the crevice in the rocks. She pushed the asparagus branch aside, and looked out, with her little hands folded about her knees. She heard the thunder rolling, and saw the red torrents rush among the stones on their way to the river. She heard the roar of the river as it now rolled, angry and red, bearing away stumps and trees on its muddy water. She listened and smiled, and pressed closer to the rock that took care of her. She pressed the palm of her hand against it. When you have no one to love you, you love the dumb things very much. When the sun set, it cleared up. Then the little girl ate some kiepersol, and lay down again to sleep. She thought there was nothing so nice as to sleep. When one has had no food but kiepersol juice for two days, one doesn't feel strong.

'It is so nice here,' she thought, as she went to sleep, 'I will stay here always.'

Afterwards the moon rose. The sky was very clear now, there was not a cloud anywhere; and the moon shone in through the bushes in the door, and made a lattice-work of light on her face. She was dreaming a beautiful dream. The loveliest dreams of all are dreamed when you are hungry. She thought she was walking in a beautiful place, holding her father's hand, and they both had crowns on their heads, crowns of wild asparagus. The people whom they passed smiled and kissed her; some gave her flowers, and some gave her food, and the sunlight was everywhere. She dreamed the same dream over and over, and it grew more and more beautiful; till, suddenly, it seemed as though she were standing quite alone. She looked up: on one side of her was a high precipice, on the other was the river, with the willow trees, drooping their branches into the water; and the moonlight was over all. Up, against the night sky the pointed leaves of the kiepersol trees were clearly marked, and the rocks and the willow trees cast dark shadows.

In her sleep she shivered, and half awoke.

'Ah! I am not there, I am here,' she said; and she crept closer to the rock, and kissed it, and went to sleep again.

It must have been about three o'clock, for the moon had begun to sink towards the western sky, when she woke, with a violent start. She sat up, and pressed her hand against her heart.

'What can it be? A coney must surely have run across my feet and frightened me!' she said, and she turned to lie down again; but soon she sat up. Outside, there was the distinct sound of thorns crackling in a fire.

She crept to the door and made an opening in the branches with her fingers.

A large fire was blazing in the shadow, at the foot of the rocks. A little Bushman sat over some burning coals that had been raked from it, cooking meat. Stretched on the ground was an Englishman, dressed in a blouse, and with a heavy, sullen face. On the stone beside him was Dirk, the Hottentot, sharpening a bowie knife.

She held her breath. Not a coney in all the rocks was so still.

'They can never find me here,' she said; and she knelt, and listened to every word they said. She could hear it all.

'You may have all the money,' said the Bushman; 'but I want the cask of brandy. I will set the roof alight in six places, for a Dutchman burnt my mother once alive in a hut, with three children.'

'You are sure there is no one else on the farm?' said the navvy.

'No, I have told you till I am tired,' said Dirk; 'the two Kaffirs have gone with the son to town; and the maids have gone to a dance; there is only the old man and the two women left.'

'But suppose,' said the navvy, 'he should have the gun at his bedside, and loaded!'

'He never has,' said Dirk; 'it hangs in the passage, and the cartridges too. He never thought when he bought it what work it was for! I only wish the little white girl was there still,' said Dirk; 'but she is drowned. We traced her footmarks to the great pool that has no bottom.'

She listened to every word, and they talked on.

Afterwards, the little Bushman, who crouched over the fire, sat up suddenly, listening.

'Ha! what is that?' he said.

A Bushman is like a dog: his ear is so fine he knows a jackal's tread from a wild dog's.

'I heard nothing,' said the navvy.

'I heard,' said the Hottentot; 'but it was only a coney on the rocks.'

'No coney, no coney,' said the Bushman; 'see, what is that there moving in the shade round the point?'

'Nothing! you idiot,' said the navvy. 'Finish your meat; we must start now.'

There were two roads to the homestead. One went along the open plain, and was by far the shortest; but you might be seen half a mile off. The other ran along the river bank, where there were rocks, and holes, and willow trees to hide among. And all down the river bank ran a little figure.

The river was swollen by the storm full to its banks, and the willow trees dipped their half-drowned branches into its water. Wherever there was a gap between them, you could see it flow, red and muddy, with the stumps upon it. But the little figure ran on and on; never looking, never thinking; panting, panting! There, where the rocks were the thickest; there, where on the open space the moonlight shone; there, where the prickly pears were tangled, and the rocks cast shadows, on it ran; the little hands clenched, the little heart beating, the eyes fixed always ahead.

It was not far to run now. Only the narrow path between the high rocks and the river.

At last she came to the end of it, and stood for an instant. Before her lay the plain, and the red farmhouse, so near, that if persons had been walking there you might have seen them in the moonlight. She clasped her hands. 'Yes, I will tell them, I will tell them!' she said; 'I am almost there!' She ran forward again, then hesitated; she shaded her eyes from the moonlight, and looked. Between her and the farmhouse there were three figures moving over the low bushes.

In the sheeny moonlight you could see how they moved on, slowly and furtively; the short one, and the one in light clothes, and the one in dark.

'I cannot help them now!' she cried, and sank down on the ground, with her little hands clasped before her.

'Awake, awake!' said the farmer's wife; 'I hear a strange noise; something calling, calling, calling!'

The man rose and went to the window.

'I hear it also,' he said; 'surely some jackal's at the sheep. I will load my gun and go and see.'

'It sounds to me like the cry of no jackal,' said the woman; and when he was gone she woke her daughter.

'Come, let us go and make a fire, I can sleep no more,' she said; 'I have heard a strange thing tonight. Your father said it was a jackal's cry, but no jackal cries so. It was a child's voice, and it cried, 'Master, master, wake!'

The women looked at each other; then they went to the kitchen, and made a great fire; and they sang psalms all the while.

At last the man came back; and they asked him, 'What have you seen?' 'Nothing,' he said, 'but the sheep asleep in their kraals, and the moonlight on the walls. And yet, it did seem to me,' he added, 'that far away near the krans by the river, I saw three figures moving. And afterwards – it might have been fancy – I thought I heard the cry again; but since that, all has been still there.'

Next day a navvy had returned to the railway works.

'Where have you been so long?' his comrades asked.

'He keeps looking over his shoulder,' said one, 'as though he thought he should see something there.'

'When he drank his grog today,' said another, 'he let it fall, and looked round.'

Next day, a small old Bushman and a Hottentot, in ragged yellow trousers, were at a wayside canteen. When the Bushman had had brandy, he began to tell how something (he did not say whether it was man, woman, or child) had lifted up its hands and cried for mercy; had kissed a white man's hands, and cried to him to help it. Then the Hottentot took the Bushman by the throat, and dragged him out.

Next night, the moon rose up, and mounted the quiet sky. She was full now, and looked in at the little home; at the purple flowers stuck about the room, and the kiepersol on the shelf. Her light fell on the willow trees, and on the high rocks, and on a little new-made heap of earth and round stones. Three men knew what was under it: and no one else ever will.

(*Lily Kloof, South Africa, 1879–80*)

2 The Lost Joy

All day, where the sunlight played on the sea-shore, Life sat.

All day the soft wind played with her hair, and the young, young face looked out across the water. She was waiting – she was waiting; but she could not tell for what.

All day the waves ran up and up on the sand, and ran back again, and the pink shells rolled. Life sat waiting; all day, with the sunlight in her eyes, she sat there, till, grown weary, she laid her head upon her knee and fell asleep, waiting still.

Then a keel grated on the sand, and then a step was on the shore – Life awoke and heard it. A hand was laid upon her, and a great shudder passed through her. She looked up, and saw over her the strange, wide eyes of Love – and Life now knew for whom she had sat there waiting.

And Love drew Life up to him.

And of that meeting was born a thing rare and beautiful – Joy, First-Joy was it called. The sunlight when it shines upon the merry water is not so glad; the rosebuds, when they turn back their lips for the sun's first kiss, are not so ruddy. Its tiny pulses beat quick. It was so warm, so soft! It never spoke, but it laughed and played in the sunshine: and Love and Life rejoiced exceedingly. Neither whispered it to the other, but deep in its own heart each said, 'It shall be ours for ever.'

Then there came a time – was it after weeks? was it after months? (Love and Life do not measure time) – when the thing was not as it had been.

Still it played; still it laughed; still it stained its mouth with purple berries; but sometimes the little hands hung weary, and the little eyes looked out heavily across the water.

And Life and Love dared not look into each other's eyes, dared not say, 'What ails our darling?' Each heart whispered to itself, 'It is nothing, it is nothing, tomorrow it will laugh out clear.' But tomorrow and tomorrow came. They journeyed on, and the child played beside them, but heavily, more heavily.

One day Life and Love lay down to sleep; and when they awoke, it was gone: only, near them, on the grass, sat a little stranger, with wide-open eyes, very soft and sad. Neither noticed it; but they walked apart, weeping bitterly, 'Oh, our Joy! our lost Joy! shall we see you no more for ever?'

The little soft and sad-eyed stranger slipped a hand into one hand of each, and drew them closer, and Life and Love walked on with it between them. And when Life looked down in anguish, she saw her tears reflected in its soft eyes. And when Love, mad with pain, cried out, 'I am weary, I am weary! I can journey no further. The light is all behind, the dark is all before,' a little rosy finger pointed where the sunlight lay upon the hillsides. Always its large eyes were sad and thoughtful: always the little brave mouth was smiling quietly.

When on the sharp stones Life cut her feet, he wiped the blood upon his garments, and kissed the wounded feet with his little lips. When in the desert Love lay down faint (for Love itself grows faint), he ran over the hot sand with his little naked feet, and even there in the desert found water in the holes in the rocks to moisten Love's lips with. He was no burden – he never weighted them; he only helped them forward on their journey.

When they came to the dark ravine where the icicles hang from the rocks – for Love and Life must pass through strange drear places – there, where all is cold, and the snow lies thick, he took their freezing hands and held them against his beating little heart, and warmed them – and softly he drew them on and on.

And when they came beyond, into the land of sunshine and flowers, strangely the great eyes lit up, and dimples broke out upon the face. Brightly laughing, it ran over the soft grass; gathered honey from the hollow tree, and brought it them on the palm of its hand; carried them water in the leaves of the lily, and gathered flowers and wreathed them round their heads, softly laughing all the while. He touched them as their Joy had touched them, but his fingers clung more tenderly.

So they wandered on, through the dark lands and the light, always with that little brave smiling one between them. Sometimes they remembered that first radiant Joy, and whispered to themselves, 'Oh! could we but find him also!'

At last they came to where Reflection sits; that strange old woman who has always one elbow on her knee, and her chin on her hand, and who steals light out of the past to shed it on the future.

And Life and Love cried out, 'O wise one! tell us: when first we met, a lovely radiant thing belonged to us – gladness without a tear, sunshine without a shade. Oh! how did we sin that we lost it? Where shall we go that we may find it?'

And she, the wise old woman, answered, 'To have it back, will you give up that which walks beside you now?'

And in agony Love and Life cried, 'No!'

'Give up this!' said Life. 'When the thorns have pierced me, who will suck the poison out? When my head throbs, who will lay his tiny hands upon it and still the beating? In the cold and the dark, who will warm my freezing heart?'

And Love cried out, 'Better let me die! Without Joy I can live; without this I cannot. Let me rather die, not lose it!'

And the wise old woman answered, 'O fools and blind! What you once had is that which you have now! When Love and Life first meet, a radiant thing is born, without a shade. When the roads begin to roughen, when the shades begin to darken, when the days are hard, and the nights cold and long – then it begins to change. Love and Life *will* not see it, *will* not know it – till one day they start up suddenly, crying, "O God! O God! we have lost it! Where is it?" They do not understand that they could not carry the laughing thing unchanged into the desert, and the frost, and the snow. They do not know that what walks beside them still is the Joy grown older. The grave, sweet, tender thing – warm in the coldest snows, brave in the dreariest deserts – its name is Sympathy; it is the Perfect Love.'

(*Begun in Hertzog, South Africa, 1871, completed at the Isle of Wight, 1881*)

3 The Wax Doll and the Stepmother

Rolly was a small boy five years old who wore knickerbockers. He had great brown eyes and curls that hung over his forehead; but Nina, his sister, who was a year older, had yellow hair and a white face. She was so thin that when Rolly tried hard he could lift her off the ground.

They had no mother, but their papa was kind to them, and one day when he came from town he brought a beautiful wax doll for Nina. She had many dolls, but none like this one. Its hair was real; you could curl and comb it as much as you pleased; it had real eyelashes, and fingers and toes of wax, and the best of all was it had little teeth. You could see them always, for its mouth was never shut.

Nurse Bromage, who looked after the children, said it was quite too good to play with, and put the doll away on the top shelf. Nina cried; she loved the doll so much, with its little teeth. But Nurse Bromage did not care; for, you see, she was a cross old thing, and didn't mind if other people weren't happy, if only she was. But sometimes she went to visit her cousin in the country, and then Jennie the housemaid used to let them play with it as much as they pleased. One day when they were playing with her one of the tucks in the doll's flannel petticoat got loosened. Nina kissed her and Rolly told her they didn't mean to do it; and so they thought it was all right.

A little time after that Nurse Bromage told them that when their papa came home the next day he was going to bring them a new mamma. The children clapped their hands when they heard that.

'Then we will have a mamma too!' they said, 'like the other children!'

'Yes,' said Nina. 'Perhaps she will come and kiss us when we are in bed, like the pretty lady kisses the little girl in the picture in papa's bedroom!'

But Nurse Bromage knit up her forehead and shook her head.

'All the house will belong to your new mamma,' she said, 'and all the things in it. She will not like you at all, because if it were not for you she would get all your papa's things when he dies; but now you will have to get some.'

Then Nina and Rolly were quite unhappy. They went and sat on a little box behind the door where they always sat when Nurse Bromage scolded them.

'We'll tell the new mamma that we don't want any of papa's things,' said Nina. 'Won't we, Rolly?'

'We'll tell her just as soon as she comes,' said Rolly. 'But perhaps she looks like Nurse Bromage!'

'Oh dear!' said Nina, and hung her head. Her neck was so thin that when she hung it, it always seemed as though it might break off.

The next day when the carriage came the servants and the two children went into the great hall to meet their papa and the lady. Nina had on a white dress with a blue sash; and Rolly had a black velvet suit with three pockets, one in the jacket and two in the trousers.

'I think she'll think I'm quite a big boy, when she sees me in this,' said Rolly.

When the carriage stopped their papa helped out the lady. She was very beautiful; tall, with red cheeks, and lips like cherries, and black hair shining like a crow's wing. She had on a silk dress with a black rustling train, and that made her grander still. She was very beautiful, but she had not a happy face. No one had ever taught her that it was not money and fine houses and fine clothes that could make a person happy; and so her heart felt all over as though it were pricked by little pins. So the hearts of all people feel, when they want more than they have got and are not full of love.

'She isn't like Nurse Bromage. She's just like your best wax doll,' Rolly whispered; but Nina was so afraid she did not lift her face.

When their new mamma came into the hall, 'These are my children,' their papa said. But she did not look at them; she only bent down and touched Rolly's forehead with her lips. Nina she did not kiss at all.

'Rolly, I can't tell her she can have all papa's things! Oh! I am so afraid of her,' said Nina, when they went up the long stairs holding each other's hands.

'*I'm* not frightened,' said Rolly, '*I'm* a *man* and you are only a woman, you know. But I don't like her. Why didn't she kiss you?'

'Oh, Rolly, I love her!' said Nina, with tears in her eyes.

That evening Nurse Bromage brought them to sit in the parlour for a little while. Their papa gave them some nuts to crack, but the beautiful lady never spoke to them; she sat with her screen before the fire.

'You see, Nina,' said Rolly, when they were lying

in their little beds in the dark, 'it is quite true; she does hate us. And I don't love her; not a bit. I'd like to take my big drum and beat it at her bedroom door when she's asleep!'

'Oh, you mustn't say so, Rolly!' said Nina. But Rolly didn't care, and soon went to sleep and so did she. But the cough soon woke her up again, and she lay alone in the dark, and a beautiful thought came to her. She wished it would be morning soon that she might tell Rolly. She folded her little hands together, and pressed the palms. For all that she couldn't tell him when the morning came, for Nurse Bromage was by, and no one could say anything nice while *she* was there. After breakfast she taught them their letters. When Nina called B, D, she whipped her hands with a little rod tied with a red string; but she didn't whip Rolly because he was her favourite.

By and by, when it was afternoon, Nurse Bromage went to sleep on the sofa. Then Nina called Rolly behind the door.

'What is it?' said Rolly, coming close and lifting his ear.

'You know my wax doll, Rolly; my best wax doll?' said Nina.

'Yes,' said Rolly.

'I want to give it to her, Rolly. Do you think she'll like it?'

'Who?'

'Our new mamma.'

'Oh, yes!' said Rolly, 'of course she will. I don't believe she ever saw one like it in her life before!'

'And you'll take it to her, Rolly? You are not afraid, are you?'

'I should think not,' said Rolly, sticking his hands into his knickerbocker pockets, and swelling himself out. 'I'll take it.'

'Let us go and fetch it before Nurse wakes,' said Nina. But Rolly paused, shaking his head and looking very sagacious.

'She'll find out and she'll whip you, Nina!'

'It doesn't matter,' said Nina, a little sorrowfully. 'You know she will whatever I do.'

So they went to the next room. Rolly pulled the chair, and Nina put the footstool on; and he climbed up, while she held fast. When he had got the doll he came down quickly; and they took a beautiful piece of white paper with a silver edge, that came with the china tea-service, to wrap it in.

'Isn't she lovely?' said Nina, as she laid it in the paper and smoothed out the little soft curls.

'She just is!' said Rolly. 'Aren't you sorry to give her away?'

'No,' said Nina; but when she looked at the little teeth her lip trembled. She gave it to Rolly to hold while she went for a piece of string. They neither of them knew how to tie a bow; but Rolly said he didn't think it mattered, because their new mamma could untie a knot by herself, he guessed.

'You must tell her I'm sorry the one tuck is out, said Nina, 'and I would have mended it only I don't know how to work.'

Rolly put the doll under his arm, and Nina went with him to the door of the long passage.

'You are not afraid, are you?'

'Oh, no!' said Rolly; but his heart beat so that the doll against his breast went up and down, up and down.

He walked up the long passage to the door of the new mamma's bedroom. He gave a little knock with his forefinger, but no one answered. He thought there could be no one inside, so gave a very brave one with his fist.

The new mamma said, 'Who is there?'

'I,' said Rolly; and he pushed open the door, and walked in.

It was almost dinner-time, and there were going to be visitors that evening. The lady was sitting before the glass dressing. She had on a black velvet dress, and the sleeves were wide open to show her arms, as white as the snow, and covered with bracelets.

Rolly walked in and stood before her looking at her.

'What do you want?' she asked.

He was such a wee boy when he stood so close beside her, and she was a grand, beautiful woman.

'I've brought this for you,' said Rolly, 'and you may keep it for your own. It's Nina sends it to you.'

He put the parcel down in her lap, and folded his hands behind him.

'And who is Nina?' asked the lady.

'Why, Nina *is* Nina, to be sure! My sister,' said Rolly. 'And she says you mustn't mind the one tuck being out, because she would have mended it if she could.'

The lady unrolled the parcel and looked at the doll.

'You see,' he said, picking up the doll's dress and showing the petticoat, 'that's the tuck; but it's all that's the matter with her. Isn't it lovely?' said Rolly, sticking his hands in his pockets and watching to see what effect it would have upon her.

'You didn't notice the teeth, I suppose, did you?' said Rolly, eyeing her critically. 'It's real teeth, and the hair too. You can put oil on if you like.'

'Who told Nina to send it?' asked the lady.

'Why, no one,' said Rolly; 'she thought of it last night when she was in bed.'

'What made her want to send it to me?'

'Well,' said Rolly, drawing confidentially nearer, 'you mustn't tell, of course; but Nina, she said if she gave it you, perhaps you'd kiss her, like the lady in the picture kisses the little girl, you know, when she's in bed.'

The lady looked down at the doll. 'Go and tell Nina, that I say "thank you."'

'It's a beautiful doll,' said Rolly, fearing she had not enough admired it, 'and the boots are red. Good-bye!'

When he got to the door he looked back. 'I'll tell her you don't mind about the petticoat, eh?'

'Yes,' said the lady, so Rolly went.

That evening the children sat on their hassocks before the fire. Nurse Bromage had taken the light out and gone downstairs to get some of the nice things that were over from the big people's dinner; so they drew their little hassocks as close together as they could and sat looking at the fire.

'She said "thank you",' said Rolly; 'she must have liked it!'

'Oh no, I think she's angry,' said Nina.

Rolly could see two large tears on her face, so he rubbed her cheeks with his coat sleeve. It was rather rough, but it did her good.

'I don't believe she could be so bad as not to like your doll,' he said; and they sat still looking at the fire.

Then the door opened softly.

'There she comes!' said Rolly, looking round – 'I knew she would.'

But the little girl sat quite huddled up with fear, and quite cold. The lady came in; you could see in the firelight how beatiful she was, with her diamonds sparkling, and her velvet dress and her black hair.

'This is Nina!' said Rolly. 'Here she sits!'

The lady did not speak. She brought the rocking-chair from the corner and put it before the fire and sat down.

'Come!' she said; and she lifted the little girl up with her strong white hands and sat her on her knee. She held the thin little face fast and kissed the mouth six times, very softly.

'My dear little daughter,' she said, and laid the head down on her breast.

Rolly, on his hassock before the fire, stroked his little knees for gladness, and his round eyes were just as bright as the coals.

The new mamma called him to come and stand at her side. She put her arm quite tight round him.

'You are just like the wax doll, and much prettier too,' he said, looking up at her. 'Nina and I, we like you very much. But I didn't like you first.'

'Why not?'

'Because – a – because – a – because – you didn't kiss her. But I like you now,' he said, edging suddenly nearer to her, and taking hold of her face with one hand to turn it to him. 'And you know, new mamma, we didn't want *any* of papa's things. You can have them all. *I'll* take care of Nina,' he added, drawing himself up; 'I'm nearly a big man already. I can climb into bed right from the ground by myself, and button my clothes too!'

'You dear little boy!' said the lady, and she kissed him on his eyes, and on his forehead, and on the brown curls that hung down.

Then Rolly put his head down on her shoulder, and rubbed his curls softly against her neck.

'It's so nice and happy; just like a birthday! Isn't it, Nina?' he said.

But Nina only pressed the lady's waist with all her little strength.

'And you won't let Nurse Bromage s-col-d Nina for giving you her doll; will you, my new mamma?' said

Rolly. 'Poor Nina, you know!'

'No one shall hurt her now,' said the lady, 'she is my little daughter.'

'Yes; and I'll be your big son too, if you like!' said Rolly, looking up, 'and take care of you!'

'So you shall, my darling.'

'Yes,' said Rolly, very much excited, 'and – I – I'll always get you – canary seed – for your bird – and – I – I'll build you a house of shells – and – and –'

'You shall do it all for me, just tomorrow,' said the lady. 'Where are your little beds? I shall carry Nina, and you shall show me. I want to undress you both.'

'Will you kiss us when we have our nightgowns on?'

'Yes.'

Rolly put his mouth close to her ear.

'Will you lie with us a little while?'

'Yes.'

'Close?'

'Yes.'

'Oh! it's just like a birthday,' said Rolly – 'only it's much nicer!'

(*South Africa, before 1881?*)

4 In a Far-off World

There is a world in one of the far-off stars, and things do not happen here as they happen there.

In that world were a man and woman; they had one work, and they walked together side by side on many days, and were friends – and that is a thing that happens now and then in this world also.

But there was something in that star-world that there is not here. There was a thick wood: where the trees grew closest, and the stems were interlocked, and the summer sun never shone, there stood a shrine. In the day all was quiet, but at night, when the stars shone or the moon glinted on the tree-tops, and all was quiet below, if one crept here quite alone and knelt on the steps of the stone altar, and uncovering one's breast, so wounded it that the blood fell down on the altar steps, then whatever he who knelt there wished for was granted him. And all this happens, as I said, because it is a far-off world, and things often happen there as they do not happen here.

Now, the man and woman walked together; and the woman wished well to the man. One night when the moon was shining so that the leaves of all the trees glinted, and the waves of the sea were silvery, the woman walked alone to the forest. It was dark there; the moonlight fell only in little flecks on the dead leaves under her feet, and the branches were knotted tight overhead. Farther in it got darker, not even a fleck of moonlight shone. Then she came to the shrine; she knelt down before it and prayed; there came no answer. Then she uncovered her breast; with a sharp two-edged stone that lay there she wounded it. The drops dripped slowly down on to the stone, and a voice cried, 'What do you seek?'

She answered, 'There is a man; I hold him nearer than anything. I would give him the best of all blessings.'

The voice said, 'What is it?'

The girl said, 'I know not, but that which is most good for him I wish him to have.'

The voice said, 'Your prayer is answered; he shall have it.'

Then she stood up. She covered her breast and held the garment tight upon it with her hand, and ran out of the forest, and the dead leaves fluttered under her feet. Out in the moonlight the soft air was blowing, and the sand glittered on the beach. She ran along the smooth shore, then suddenly she stood still. Out across the water there was something moving. She shaded her eyes and looked. It was a boat; it was sliding swiftly over the moonlit water out to sea. One stood upright in it; the face the moonlight did not show, but the figure she knew. It was passing swiftly; it seemed as if no one propelled it; the moonlight's shimmer did not let her see clearly, and the boat was far from shore, but it seemed almost as if there was another figure sitting in the stern. Faster and faster it glided over the water away, away. She ran along the shore; she came no nearer it. The garment she had held closed fluttered open; she stretched out her arms, and the moonlight shone on her long loose hair.

Then a voice beside her whispered, 'What is it?'

She cried, 'With my blood I bought the best of all gifts for him. I have come to bring it him! He is going from me!'

The voice whispered softly, 'Your prayer was answered. It has been given him.'

She cried, 'What is it?'

The voice answered, 'It is that he might leave you.'

The girl stood still.

Far out at sea the boat was lost to sight beyond the moonlight sheen.

The voice spoke softly, 'Art thou contented?'

She said, 'I am contented.'

At her feet the waves broke in long ripples softly on the shore.

(*Alassio, Italy, 1887*)

5 The Buddhist Priest's Wife

Cover her up! How still it lies! You can see the outline under the white. You would think she was asleep. Let the sunshine come in; it loved it so. She that had travelled so far, in so many lands, and done so much and seen so much, how she must like rest now! Did she ever love anything absolutely, this woman whom so many men loved, and so many women; who gave so much sympathy and never asked for anything in return! did she ever need a love she could not have? Was she never obliged to unclasp her fingers from anything to which they clung? Was she really so strong as she looked? Did she never wake up in the night crying for that which she could not have? Were thought and travel enough for her? Did she go about for long days with a weight that crushed her to earth? Cover her up! I do not think she would have liked us to look at her. In one way she was alone all her life; she would have liked to be alone now. . ! Life must have been very beautiful to her, or she would not look so young now. Cover her up! Let us go!

Many years ago in a London room, up long flights of

stairs, a fire burnt up in a grate. It showed the marks on the walls where pictures had been taken down, and the little blue flowers in the wallpaper and the blue felt carpet on the floor, and a woman sat by the fire in a chair at one side.

Presently the door opened, and the old woman came in who took care of the entrance hall downstairs.

'Do you not want anything tonight?' she said.

'No, I am only waiting for a visitor; when they have been, I shall go.'

'Have you got all your things taken away already?'

'Yes, only these I am leaving.'

The old woman went down again, but presently came up with a cup of tea in her hand.

'You must drink that; it's good for one. Nothing helps one like tea when one's been packing all day.'

The young woman at the fire did not thank her, but she ran her hand over the old woman's from the wrist to the fingers.

'I'll say goodbye to you when I go out.'

The woman poked the fire, put the last coals on, and went.

When she had gone the young one did not drink the tea, but drew her little silver cigarette case from her pocket and lighted a cigarette. For a while she sat smoking by the fire; then she stood up and walked the room.

When she had paced for a while she sat down again beside the fire. She threw the end of her cigarette away into the fire, and then began to walk again with her hands behind her. Then she went back to her seat and lit another cigarette, and paced again. Presently she sat down, and looked into the fire; she pressed the palms of her hands together, and then sat quietly staring into it.

Then there was a sound of feet on the stairs and someone knocked at the door.

She rose and threw the end into the fire and said without moving, 'Come in.'

The door opened and a man stood there in evening dress. He had a greatcoat on, open in front.

'May I come in? I couldn't get rid of this downstairs; I didn't see where to leave it!' He took his coat off. 'How are you? This is a real bird's nest!'

She motioned to a chair.

'I hope you did not mind my asking you to come?'

'Oh no, I am delighted. I only found your note at my club twenty minutes ago.'

He sat down on a chair before the fire.

'So you really are going to India? How delightful! But what are you to do there? I think it was Grey told me six weeks ago you were going, but regarded it as one of those mythical stories which don't deserve credence. Yet I'm sure I don't know! Why, nothing would surprise me.'

He looked at her in a half-amused, half-interested way.

'What a long time it is since we met! Six months, eight?'

'Seven,' she said.

'I really thought you were trying to avoid me. What have you been doing with yourself all this time?'

'Oh, been busy. Won't you have a cigarette?'

She held out the little case to him.

'Won't you take one yourself? I know you object to smoking with men, but you can make an exception in my case!'

'Thank you.' She lit her own and passed him the matches.

'But really what have you been doing with yourself all this time? You've entirely disappeared from civilized life. When I was down at the Grahams' in the spring, they said you were coming down there, and then at the last moment cried off. We were all quite disappointed. What is taking you to India now? Going to preach the doctrine of social and intellectual equality to the Hindu women and incite them to revolt? Marry some old Buddhist priest, build a little cottage on the top of the Himalayas and live there, discuss philosophy and meditate? I believe that's what you'd like. I really shouldn't wonder if I heard you'd done it!'

She laughed and took out her cigarette case.

She smoked slowly.

'I've been here a long time, four years, and I want change. I was glad to see how well you succeeded in that election,' she said. 'You were much interested in it, were you not?'

'Oh, yes. We had a stiff fight. It tells in my favour, you know, though it was not exactly a personal matter. But it was a great worry.'

'Don't you think,' she said, 'you were wrong in sending that letter to the papers? It would have strengthened your position to have remained silent.'

'Yes, perhaps so; I think so now, but I did it under advice. However, we've won, so it's all right.' He leaned back in the chair.

'Are you pretty fit?'

'Oh, yes; pretty well; bored, you know. One doesn't know what all this working and striving is for sometimes.'

'Where are you going for your holiday this year?'

'Oh, Scotland, I suppose; I always do; the old quarters.'

'Why don't you go to Norway? It would be more change for you and rest you more. Did you get a book on sport in Norway?'

'Did you send it me? How kind of you! I read it with much interest. I was almost inclined to start off there and then. I suppose it is the kind of *vis inertiae* that creeps over one as one grows older that sends one back to the old place. A change would be much better.'

'There's a list at the end of the book,' she said, 'of exactly the things one needs to take. I thought it would save trouble; you could just give it to your man, and let him get them all. Have you still got him?'

'Oh, yes. He's as faithful to me as a dog. I think nothing would induce him to leave me. He won't allow me to go out hunting since I sprained my foot last autumn. I have to do it surreptitiously. He thinks I can't keep my seat with a sprained ankle; but he's a very good fellow; takes care of me like a mother.' He smoked quietly with the firelight glowing on his black coat. 'But what are you going to India for? Do you know anyone there?'

'No,' she said. 'I think it will be so splendid. I've always been a great deal interested in the East. It's a complex, interesting life.'

He turned and looked at her.

'Going to seek for more experience, you'll say, I suppose. I never knew a woman throw herself away as you do; a woman with your brilliant parts and attractions, to let the whole of life slip through your hands, and make nothing of it. You ought to be the most successful woman in London. Oh, yes; I know what you are going to say: "You don't care." That's just it; you don't. You are always going to get experience, going to get everything, and you never do. You are always going to write when you know enough, and you are never satisfied that you do. You ought to be making your two thousand a year, but you don't care. That's just it! Living, burying yourself here with a lot of old frumps. You will never do anything. You could have everything and you let it slip.'

'Oh, my life is very full,' she said. 'There are only two things that are absolute realities, love and knowledge, and you can't escape them.'

She had thrown her cigarette end away and was looking into the fire, smiling.

'I've let these rooms to a woman friend of mine.' She glanced round the room, smiling. 'She doesn't know I'm going to leave these things here for her. She'll like them because they were mine. The world's very beautiful, I think – delicious.'

'Oh, yes. But what do you do with it? What do you make of it? You ought to settle down and marry like other women, not go wandering about the world to India and China and Italy, and God knows where. You are simply making a mess of your life. You're always surrounding yourself with all sorts of extraordinary people. If I hear any man or woman is a great friend of yours, I always say: "What's the matter? Lost his money? Lost his character? Got an incurable disease?" I believe the only way in which anyone becomes interesting to you is by having some complaint of mind or body. I believe you worship rags. To come and shut yourself up in a place like this away from everybody and everything! It's a mistake; it's idiotic, you know.'

'I'm very happy,' she said. 'You see,' she said, leaning forwards towards the fire with her hands on her knees, 'what matters is that something should need you. It isn't a question of love. What's the use of being near a thing if other people could serve it as well as you can? If they could serve it better, it's pure selfishness. It's the need of one thing for another that makes the organic bond of union. You love mountains and horses, but they don't need you; so what's the use of saying anything about it! I suppose the most absolutely delicious thing in life is to feel a thing needs you, and to give at the moment it needs. Things that don't need you, you must love from a distance.'

'Oh, but a woman like you ought to marry, ought to have children. You go squandering yourself on every old beggar or forlorn female or escaped criminal you meet; it may be very nice for them, but it's a mistake from your point of view.'

He touched the ash gently with the tip of his little finger and let it fall.

'I intend to marry. It's a curious thing,' he said, resuming his pose with an elbow on one knee and his head bent forward on one side, so that she saw the brown hair with its close curls a little tinged with grey at the sides, 'that when a man reaches a certain age he wants to marry. He doesn't fall in love; it's not that he definitely plans anything; but he has a feeling that he ought to have a home and a wife and children. I suppose it is the same kind of feeling that makes a bird build nests at certain times of the year. It's not love; it's something else. When I was a young man I used to despise men for getting married; wondered what they did it for; they had everything to lose and nothing to gain. But when a man gets to be six-and-thirty his feeling changes. It's not love, passion, he wants; it's a home; it's a wife and children. He may have a house and servants; it isn't the same thing. I should have thought a woman would have felt it too.'

She was quiet for a minute, holding a cigarette between her fingers; then she said slowly:

'Yes, at times a woman has a curious longing to have a child, especially when she gets near to thirty or over it. It's something distinct from love for any definite person. But it's a thing one has to get over. For a woman, marriage is much more serious than for a man. She might pass her life without meeting a man whom she could possibly love, and, if she met him, it might not be right or possible. Marriage has become very complex now it has become so largely intellectual. Won't you have another?'

She held out the case to him. 'You can light it from mine.' She bent forward for him to light it.

'You are a man who ought to marry. You've no absorbing mental work with which the woman would interfere; it would complete you.' She sat back, smoking serenely.

'Yes,' he said, 'but life is too busy; I never find time to look for one, and I haven't a fancy for the pink-and-white prettiness so common and that some men like so. I need something else. If I am to have a wife I shall have to go to America to look for one.'

'Yes, an American would suit you best.'

'Yes,' he said, 'I don't want a woman to look after; she must be self-sustaining and she mustn't bore you. You know what I mean. Life is too full of cares to have a helpless child added to them.'

'Yes,' she said, standing up and leaning with her elbow against the fireplace. 'The kind of woman you want would be young and strong, she need not be excessively beautiful, but she must be attractive; she must have energy, but not too strongly marked an individuality; she must be largely neutral; she need not give you too passionate or too deep a devotion, but she must second you in a thoroughly rational manner. She must have the same aims and tastes that you have. No woman has the right to marry a man if she has to bend herself out of shape for him. She might wish to, but she could never be to him with all her passionate endeavour what the other woman could be to him without trying. Character will dominate over all and will come out at last.'

She looked down into the fire.

'When you marry you mustn't marry a woman who flatters you too much. It is always a sign of falseness somewhere. If a woman absolutely loves you as herself, she will criticize and understand you as herself. Two people who are to live through life together must be able to look into each other's eyes and speak the truth. That helps one through life. You would find many such women in America,' she said, 'women who would help you to succeed, who would not drag you down.'

'Yes, that's my idea. But how am I to obtain the ideal woman?'

'Go and look for her. Go to America instead of Scotland this year. It is perfectly right. A man has a right to look for what he needs. With a woman it is different. That's one of the radical differences between men and women.'

She looked downwards into the fire.

'It's a law of her nature and of sex relationship. There's nothing arbitrary or conventional about it any more than there is in her having to bear her child while the male does not. Intellectually we may both be alike. I suppose if fifty men and fifty women had to solve a mathematical problem, they would all do it in the same way; the more abstract and intellectual, the more alike we are. The nearer you approach to the personal and sexual, the more different we are. If I were to represent men's and women's natures,' she said, 'by a diagram, I would take two circular discs; the right side of each I should paint bright red; then I would shade the red away till in a spot on the left edge it became blue in the one and green in the other. That spot represents sex, and the nearer you come to it, the more the two discs differ in colour. Well then, if you turn them so that the red sides touch, they seem to be exactly alike, but if you turn them so that the green and blue paint form their point of contact, they will seem to be entirely unlike. That's why you notice the brutal, sensual men invariably believe women are entirely different from men, another species of creature; and very cultured, intellectual men sometimes believe we are exactly alike. You see, sex love in its substance may be the same in both of us; in the form of its expression it must differ. It is not man's fault; it is nature's. If a man loves a woman, he has a right to try to make her love him because he can do it openly, directly, without bending. There need be no subtlety, no directness. With a woman it's not so; she can take no love that is not laid openly, simply, at her feet. Nature ordains that she should never show what she feels; the woman who had told a man she loved him would have put between them a barrier once and for ever that could not be crossed; and if she subtly drew him towards her, using the woman's means – silence, finesse, the dropped handkerchief, the surprise visit, the gentle assertion she had not thought to see him when she had come a long way to meet him, then she would be damned; she would hold the love, but she would have desecrated it by subtlety; it would have no value. Therefore she must always go with her arms folded sexually; only the love which lays itself down at her feet and implores of her to accept it is love she can ever rightly take up. That is the true difference between a man and a woman. You may seek for love because you can do it openly; we cannot because we must do it subtly. A woman should always walk with her arms folded. Of course friendship is different. You are on a perfect equality with man then; you can ask him to come and see you as I asked you. That's the beauty of the intellect and intellectual life to a woman, that she drops her shackles a little; and that is why she shrinks from sex so. If she were dying perhaps, or doing something equal to death, she might. . . Death means so much more to a woman than a man; when you knew you were dying, to look round on the world and feel the bond of sex that has broken and crushed you all your life gone, nothing but the human left, no woman any more, to meet everything on perfectly even ground. There's no reason why you shouldn't go to America and look for a wife perfectly deliberately. You will have to tell no lies. Look till you find a woman that you absolutely love, that you have not the smallest doubt suits you apart from love, and then ask her to marry you. You must have children; the life of an old childless man is very sad.'

'Yes, I should like to have children. I often feel now, what is it all for, this work, this striving, and no one to leave it to? It's a blank, suppose I succeed. . ?'

'Suppose you get your title?'

'Yes; what is it all worth to me if I've no one to leave it to? That's my feeling. It's really very strange to be sitting and talking like this to you. But you are so different from other women. If all women were like you, all your theories of the equality of men and women would work. You're the only woman with whom I never realize that she is a woman.'

'Yes,' she said.

She stood looking down into the fire.

'How long will you stay in India?'

'Oh, I'm not coming back.'

'Not coming back! That's impossible. You will be breaking the hearts of half the people here if you don't. I never knew a woman who had such power of entrapping men's hearts as you have in spite of that philosophy of yours. I don't know,' he smiled, 'that I should not have fallen into the snare myself — three years ago I almost thought I should – if you hadn't always attacked me so incontinently and persistently on all and every point and on each and every occasion. A man doesn't like pain. A succession of slaps damps him. But it doesn't seem to have that effect on other men. . . There was that fellow down in the country when I was there last year, perfectly ridiculous. You know his name. . .' He moved his fingers to try and remember it – 'big, yellow moustache, a major, gone to the east coast of Africa now; the ladies unearthed it that he was always carrying about a photograph of yours in his pocket; and he used to take out little scraps of things you printed and show them to people mysteriously. He almost had a duel with a man one night after dinner because he mentioned you; he seemed to think there was something incongruous between your name and –'

'I do not like to talk of any man who has loved me,' she said. 'However small and poor his nature may be, he has given me his best. There is nothing ridiculous in love. I think a woman should feel that all the love men have given her which she has not been able to return is a kind of crown set up above her which she is always trying to grow tall enough to wear. I can't bear to think that all the love that has been given me has been wasted on something unworthy of it. Men have been very beautiful and greatly honoured me. I am grateful to them. If a man tells you he loves you,' she said, looking into the fire, 'with his breast uncovered before you for you to strike him if you will, the least you can do is to put out your hand and cover it up from other people's eyes. If I were a deer,' she said, 'and a stag got hurt following me, even though I could not have him for a companion, I would stand still and scrape the sand with my foot over the place where his blood had fallen; the rest of the herd should never know he had been hurt there following me. I would cover the blood up, if I were a deer,' she said, and then she was silent.

Presently she sat down in her chair and said, with her hand before her: 'Yet, you know, I have not the ordinary feeling about love. I think the one who is loved confers the benefit on the one who loves, it's been so great and beautiful that it should be loved. I think the man should be grateful to the woman or the woman to the man whom they have been able to love, whether they have been loved back or whether circumstances have divided them or not.' She stroked her knee softly with her hand.

'Well, really, I must go now.' He pulled out his watch. 'It's so fascinating sitting here talking that I could stay all night, but I've still two engagements.' He rose; she rose also and stood before him looking up at him for a moment.

'How well you look! I think you have found the secret of perpetual youth. You don't look a day older than when I first saw you just four years ago. You always look as if you were on fire and being burnt up, but you never are, you know.'

He looked down at her with a kind of amused face as one does at an interesting child or a big Newfoundland dog.

'When shall we see you back?'

'Oh, not at all!'

'Not at all! Oh, we must have you back; you belong here, you know. You'll get tired of your Buddhist and come back to us.'

'You didn't mind my asking you to come and say goodbye?' she said in a childish manner unlike her determinateness when she discussed anything impersonal. 'I wanted to say goodbye to everyone. If one hasn't said goodbye one feels restless and feels one would have to come back. If one has said goodbye to all one's friends, then one knows it is all ended.'

'Oh, this isn't a final farewell! You must come in ten years' time and we'll compare notes – you about your Buddhist priest, I about my fair ideal American; and we'll see who succeeded best.'

She laughed.

'I shall always see your movements chronicled in the newspapers, so we shall not be quite sundered; and you will hear of me perhaps.'

'Yes, I hope you will be very successful.'

She was looking at him, with her eyes wide open, from head to foot. He turned to the chair where his coat hung.

'Can't I help you put it on?'

'Oh, no, thank you.'

He put it on.

'Button the throat,' she said, 'the room is warm.'

He turned to her in his greatcoat and with his gloves. They were standing near the door.

'Well, goodbye. I hope you will have a very pleasant time.'

He stood looking down upon her, wrapped in his greatcoat.

She put up one hand a little in the air. 'I want to ask you something,' she said quickly.

'Well, what is it?'

'Will you please kiss me?'

For a moment he looked down at her, then he bent over her.

In after years he could never tell certainly, but he always thought she put up her hand and rested it on the crown of his head, with a curious soft caress, something like a mother's touch when her child is asleep and she does not want to wake it. Then he looked round, and she was gone. The door had closed noiselessly. For a moment he stood motionless, then he walked to the fireplace and looked down into the fender at a little cigarette end lying there, then he walked quickly back to the door and opened it. The stairs were in darkness and silence. He rang the bell violently. The old woman came up. He asked her where the lady was. She said she had gone out, she had a cab waiting. He asked when she would be back. The old woman said, 'Not at all'; she had left. He asked where she had gone. The woman said she did not know; she had left orders that all her letters should be kept for six or eight months till she wrote and sent her address. He asked whether she had no idea where he might find her. The woman said no. He walked up to a space in the wall where a picture had hung and stood staring at it as though the picture were still hanging there. He drew his mouth as though he were emitting a long whistle, but no sound came. He gave the old woman ten shillings and went downstairs.

That was eight years ago.

How beautiful life must have been to it that it looks so young still!

(*Matjiesfontein, South Africa, 1891–92*)

6 I Thought I Stood

1

I thought I stood in heaven before God's throne, and God asked me what I had come for. I said I had come to arraign my brother, Man.

God said, 'What has he done?'

I said, 'He has taken my sister, Woman, and has stricken her, and wounded her, and thrust her out into the streets; she lies there prostrate. His hands are red with blood. *I* am here to arraign him; that the kingdom be taken from him, because he is not worthy, and given unto me. My hands are pure.'

I showed them.

God said, 'Thy hands are pure. Lift up thy robe.'

I raised it; my feet were red, blood-red, as if I had trodden in wine.

God said, 'How is this?'

I said, 'Dear Lord, the streets on earth are full of mire. If I should walk straight on in them my outer robe might be bespotted, you see how white it is! Therefore I pick my way.'

God said, '*On what*?'

I was silent, and I let my robe fall. I wrapped my mantle about my head. I went out softly. I was afraid that the angels would see me.

2

Once more I stood at the gate of Heaven, I and another. We held fast by one another; we were very tired. We looked up at the great gates; the angels opened them, and we went in. The mud was on our garments. We walked across the marble floor, and up to the great throne. Then the angels divided us. Her, they set upon the top step, but me, upon the bottom; for, they said, 'Last time this woman came here she left red footmarks on the floor; we had to wash them out with our tears. Let her not go up.'

Then she, with whom I came, looked back, and stretched out her hand to me; and I went and stood beside her. And the angels, they, the shining ones who never sinned and never suffered, walked by us to and fro and up and down; I think we should have felt a little lonely there if it had not been for one another, the angels were so bright.

God asked me what I had come for; and I drew my sister forward a little that he might see her.

God said, 'How is it you are here together today?'

I said, 'She was upon the ground in the street, and they passed over her; I lay down by her, and she put her arms around my neck, and so I lifted her, and we two rose together.'

God said, 'Whom are you now come to accuse before me?'

I said, 'We are come to accuse no man.'

And God bent, and said, 'My children – what is it that ye seek?'

And she beside me drew my hand that I should speak for both.

I said, 'We have come to ask that thou shouldst speak to Man, our brother, and give us a message for him that he might understand, and that he might –'

God said, 'Go, take the message down to him!'

I said, 'But what *is* the message?'

God said, 'Upon your hearts it is written; take it down to him.'

And we turned to go; the angels went with us to the door. They looked at us.

And one said – 'Ai! but their dresses are beautiful!'

And the other said, 'I thought it was mire when they came in, but see, it is all golden!'

But another said, 'Hush, it is the light from their faces!'

And we went down to him.

(*Alassio, Italy, 1886–87*)

7 The Woman's Rose

I have an old, brown, carved box; the lid is broken and tied with a string. In it I keep little squares of paper, with hair inside, and a little picture which hung over my brother's bed when we were children, and other things as small. I have in it a rose. Other women also have such boxes where they keep such trifles, but no one has my rose.

When my eye is dim, and my heart grows faint, and my faith in woman flickers, and her present is an agony to me, and her future a despair, the scent of that dead rose, withered for twelve years, comes back to me. I know there will be spring; as surely as the birds know it when they see above the snow two tiny, quivering green leaves. Spring cannot fail us.

There were other flowers in the box once; a bunch of white acacia flowers, gathered by the strong hand of a man, as we passed down a village street on a sultry afternoon, when it had rained, and the drops fell on us from the leaves of the acacia trees. The flowers were damp; they made mildew marks on the paper I folded them in. After many years I threw them away. There is nothing of them left in the box now, but a faint, strong smell of dried acacia, that recalls that sultry summer afternoon; but the rose is in the box still.

It is many years ago now; I was a girl of fifteen, and I went to visit in a small up-country town. It was young in those days, and two days' journey from the nearest village; the population consisted mainly of men. A few were married, and had their wives and children, but most were single. There was only one young girl there when I came. She was about seventeen, fair, and rather fully fleshed; she had large dreamy blue eyes, and wavy light hair; full, rather heavy lips, until she smiled; then her face broke into dimples, and all her white teeth shone. The hotel-keeper may have had a daughter, and the farmer in the outskirts had two, but we never saw them. She reigned alone. All the men worshipped her. She was the only woman they had to think of. They talked of her on the stoep, at the market, at the hotel; they watched for her at street corners; they hated the man she bowed to or walked with down the street. They brought flowers to the front door; they offered her their horses; they begged her to marry them when they dared. Partly, there was something noble and heroic in this devotion of men to the best woman they knew; partly there was something natural in it, that these men, shut off from the world, should pour at the feet of one woman the worship that otherwise would have been given to twenty; and partly there was something mean in their envy of one another. If she had raised her little finger, I suppose, she might have married any one out of twenty of them.

Then I came. I do not think I was prettier; I do not think I was so pretty as she was. I was certainly not as handsome. But I was vital, and I was new, and she was old – they all forsook her and followed me. They worshipped me. It was to my door that the flowers came; it was I had twenty horses offered me when I could only ride one; it was for me they waited at street corners; it was what I said and did that they talked of. Partly I liked it. I had lived alone all my life; no one ever had told me I was beautiful and a woman. I believed them. I did not know it was simply a fashion, which one man had set and the rest followed unreasoningly. I liked them to ask me to marry them, and to say, No. I despised them. The mother heart had not swelled in me yet; I did not know all men were my children, as the large woman knows when her heart is grown. I was too small to be tender. I liked my power. I was like a child with a new whip, which it goes about cracking everywhere, not caring against what. I could not wind it up and put it away. Men were curious creatures, who liked me, I could never tell why. Only one thing took from my pleasure; I could not bear that they had deserted her for me. I liked her dreamy blue eyes, I liked her slow walk and drawl; when I saw her sitting among men, she seemed to me much too good to be among them; I would have given all their compliments if she would once have smiled at me as she smiled at them, with all her face breaking into radiance, with her dimples and flashing teeth. But I knew it never could be; I felt sure she hated me; that she wished I was dead; that she wished I had never come to the village. She did not know, when we went out riding, and a man who had always ridden beside her came to ride beside me, that I sent him away; that once when a man thought to win my favour by ridiculing her slow drawl before me, I turned on him so fiercely that he never dared come before me again. I knew she knew that at the hotel men had made a bet as to which was the prettier, she or I, and had asked each man who came in, and that the one who had staked on me won. I hated them for it, but

I would not let her see that I cared about what she felt towards me.

She and I never spoke to each other.

If we met in the village street we bowed and passed on; when we shook hands we did so silently, and did not look at each other. But I thought she felt my presence in a room just as I felt hers.

At last the time for my going came. I was to leave the next day. Someone I knew gave a party in my honour, to which all the village was invited.

It was midwinter; there was nothing in the gardens but a few dahlias and chrysanthemums, and I suppose that for two hundred miles round there was not a rose to be bought for love or money. Only in the garden of a friend of mine, in a sunny corner between the oven and the brick wall, there was a rose-tree growing which had on it one bud. It was white, and it had been promised to the fair-haired girl to wear at the party.

The evening came; when I arrived and went to the waiting-room, to take off my mantle, I found the girl there already. She was dressed in pure white, with her great white arms and shoulders showing, and her bright hair glittering in the candle-light, and the white rose fastened at her breast. She looked like a queen. I said, 'Good evening,' and turned away quickly to the glass to arrange my old black scarf across my old black dress.

Then I felt a hand touch my hair.

'Stand still,' she said.

I looked in the glass. She had taken the white rose from her breast, and was fastening it in my hair.

'How nice dark hair is! it sets off flowers so.' She stepped back and looked at me. 'It looks much better there!'

I turned round.

'You are so beautiful to me,' I said.

'Y-e-s,' she said, with her slow colonial drawl; 'I'm so glad.'

We stood looking at each other.

Then they came in and swept us away to dance. All the evening we did not come near each other. Only once, as she passed, she smiled at me.

The next morning I left the town.

I never saw her again.

Years afterwards I heard she had married and gone to America; it may or may not be so – but the rose – the rose is in the box still! When my faith in woman grows dim, and it seems that for want of love and magnanimity she can play no part in any future heaven; then the scent of that small withered thing comes back: – spring cannot fail us.

(*Matjiesfontein, South Africa, 1890–91*)

8 In a Ruined Chapel

'I cannot forgive – I love.'

There are four bare walls; there is a Christ upon the walls, in red, carrying his cross; there is a Blessèd Bambino with the face rubbed out; there is a madonna in blue and red; there are Roman soldiers and a Christ with tied hands. All the roof is gone; overhead is the blue, blue Italian sky; the rain has beaten holes in the walls, and the plaster is peeling from it. The chapel stands here alone upon the promontory, and by day and by night the sea breaks at its feet. Some say that it was set here by the monks from the island down below, that they might bring their sick here in times of deadly plague. Some say that it was set here that the passing monks and friars, as they hurried by upon the roadway, might stop and say their prayers here. Now no one stops to pray here, and the sick come no more to be healed.

Behind it runs the old Roman road. If you climb it and come and sit there alone on a hot sunny day you may almost hear at last the clink of the Roman soldiers upon the pavement, and the sound of that older time, as you sit there in the sun, when Hannibal and his men broke through the brushwood, and no road was.

Now it is very quiet. Sometimes a peasant girl comes riding by between her panniers, and you hear the mule's feet beat upon the bricks of the pavement; sometimes an old woman goes past with a bundle of weeds upon her head, or a brigand-looking man hurries by with a bundle of sticks in his hand; but for the rest the chapel lies here alone upon the promontory, between the two bays, and hears the sea break at its feet.

I came here one winter's day when the midday sun shone hot on the bricks of the Roman road. I was weary, and the way seemed steep. I walked into the chapel to the broken window, and looked out across the bay. Far off, across the blue, blue water, were towns and villages, hanging white and red dots, upon the mountainsides, and the blue mountains rose up into the sky, and now stood out from it and now melted back again.

The mountains seemed calling to me, but I knew there would never be a bridge built from them to me; never, never, never! I shaded my eyes with my hand and turned away. I could not bear to look at them.

I walked through the ruined chapel, and looked at the Christ in red carrying his cross, and the Blessèd rubbed-out Bambino, and the Roman soldiers, and the folded hands, and the reed; and I went and sat down in the open porch upon a stone. At my feet was the small bay, with its white row of houses buried among the olive trees; the water broke in a long, thin, white line of foam along the shore; and I leaned my elbows on my knees. I was tired, very tired; tired with a tiredness that seemed older than the heat of the day and the shining of the sun on the bricks of the Roman road; and I lay my head upon my knees; I heard the breaking of the water on the rocks three hundred feet below, and the rustling of the wind among the olive trees and the ruined arches, and then I fell asleep there. I had a dream.

A man cried up to God, and God sent down an angel to help him; and the angel came back and said, 'I cannot help that man.'

God said, 'How is it with him?'

And the angel said, 'He cries out continually that one has injured him; and he would forgive him and he cannot.'

God said, 'What have you done for him?'

The angel said, 'All —. I took him by the hand, and I said, "See, when other men speak ill of that man do you speak well of him; secretly, in ways he shall not know, serve him; if you have anything you value share it with him, so, serving him, you will at last come to feel possession in him, and you will forgive." And he said, "I will do it." Afterwards, as I passed by in the dark of night, I heard one crying out, "I have done all. It helps nothing! My speaking well of him helps me nothing! If I share my heart's blood with him, is the burning within me less? I cannot forgive; I cannot forgive! Oh, God, I cannot forgive!"

'I said to him, "See here, look back on all your past. See from your childhood all smallness, all indirectness that has been yours; look well at it, and in its light do you not see every man your brother? Are you so sinless you have right to hate?"

'He looked, and said, "Yes, you are right; I too have failed, and I forgive my fellow. Go, I am satisfied. I have forgiven"; and he laid him down peacefully and folded his hands on his breast, and I thought it was well with him. But scarcely had my wings rustled and I turned to come up here, when I heard one crying out on earth again, "I cannot forgive! I cannot forgive! Oh, God, God, I cannot forgive! It is better to die than to hate! I cannot forgive! I cannot forgive!" And I went and stood outside his door in the dark, and I heard him cry, "I have not sinned so, not so! If I have torn my fellows' flesh ever so little, I have kneeled down and kissed the wound with my mouth till it was healed. I have not willed that any soul should be lost through hate of me. If they have but fancied that I wronged them I have lain down on the ground before them that they might tread on me, and so, seeing my humiliation, forgive and not be lost through hating me; they have not cared that my soul should be lost; they have not willed to save me; they have not tried that I should forgive them!"

'I said to him, "See here, be thou content; do *not* forgive: forget this soul and its injury; go on your way. In the next world perhaps –"

'He cried, "Go from me, you understand nothing! What is the next world to me! I am lost now, today. I cannot see the sunlight shine, the dust is in my throat, the sand is in my eyes! Go from me, you know nothing! Oh, once again before I die to see that the world is beautiful! Oh, God, God, I cannot live and not love. I cannot live and hate. Oh, God, God, God!" So I left him crying out and came back here.'

God said, 'This man's soul must be saved.'

And the angel said, 'How?'

God said, 'Go down you, and save it.'

The angel said, 'What more shall I do?'

Then God bent down and whispered in the angel's ear, and the angel spread out its wings and went down to earth.

And partly I woke, sitting there upon the broken

stone with my head on my knee; but I was too weary to rise. I heard the wind roam through the olive trees and among the ruined arches, and then I slept again.

The angel went down and found the man with the bitter heart and took him by the hand, and led him to a certain spot.

Now the man wist not where it was the angel would take him nor what he would show him there. And when they came the angel shaded the man's eyes with his wing, and when he moved it the man saw somewhat on the earth before them. For God had given it to that angel to unclothe a human soul; to take from it all those outward attributes of form, and colour, and age, and sex, whereby one man is known from among his fellows and is marked off from the rest, and the soul lay before them, bare, as a man turning his eye inwards beholds himself.

They saw its past, its childhood, the tiny life with the dew upon it; they saw its youth when the dew was melting, and the creature raised its lilliputian mouth to drink from a cup too large for it, and they saw how the water spilt; they saw its hopes that were never realized; they saw its hours of intellectual blindness, men call sin; they saw its hours of all-radiating insight, which men call righteousness; they saw its hour of strength, when it leaped to its feet crying, 'I am omnipotent'; its hour of weakness, when it fell to the earth and grasped dust only; they saw what it might have been, but never would be.

The man bent forward.

And the angel said, 'What is it?'

He answered, 'It is *I!* it is myself!'

And he went forward as if he would have lain his heart against it; but the angel held him back and covered his eyes.

Now God had given power to the angel further to unclothe that soul, to take from it all those outward attributes of time and place and circumstance whereby the individual life is marked off from the life of the whole.

Again the angel uncovered the man's eyes, and he looked. He saw before him that which in its tiny drop reflects the whole universe; he saw that which marks within itself the step of the furthest star, and tells how the crystal grows underground where no eye has seen it; that which is where the germ in the egg stirs; which moves the outstretched fingers of the little newborn babe, and keeps the leaves of the trees pointing upward; which moves where the jellyfish sail alone on the sunny seas, and is where the lichens form on the mountains' rocks.

And the man looked.

And the angel touched him.

But the man bowed his head and shuddered. He whispered – '*It is God!*'

And the angel re-covered the man's eyes. And when he uncovered them there was one walking from them a little way off – for the angel had re-clothed the soul in its outward form and vesture – and the man knew who it was.

And the angel said, 'Do you know him?'

And the man said, 'I know him,' and he looked after the figure.

And the angel said, 'Have you forgiven him?'

But the man said, '*How beautiful my brother is!*'

And the angel looked into the man's eyes, and he shaded his own face with his wing from the light. He laughed softly and went up to God.

But the men were together on earth.

I awoke.

The blue, blue sky was over my head, and the waves were breaking below on the shore. I walked through the little chapel, and I saw the madonna in blue and red, and the Christ carrying his cross, and the Roman soldiers with the rod, and the Blessèd Bambino with its broken face; and then I walked down the sloping rock to the brick pathway. The olive trees stood up on either side of the road, their black berries and pale-green leaves stood out against the sky; and the little ice-plants hung from the crevices in the stone wall. It seemed to me as if it must have rained while I was asleep. I thought I had never seen the heavens and the earth look so beautiful before. I walked down the road. The old, old, old tiredness was gone.

Presently there came a peasant boy down the path leading his ass; she had two large panniers fastened to her sides, and they went down the road before me.

I had never seen him before; but I should have liked to walk by him and to have held his hand – only, he would not have known why.

(*Alassio, Italy, 1887*)

9 The Policy in Favour of Protection

Was it Right? – Was it Wrong?

A woman sat at her desk in the corner of a room; behind her a fire burnt brightly.

Presently a servant came in and gave her a card.

'Say I am busy and can see no one now. I have to finish this article by two o'clock.'

The servant came back. The caller said she would only keep her a moment: it was necessary she should see her.

The woman rose from her desk. 'Tell the boy to wait. Ask the lady to come in.'

A young woman in a silk dress, with a cloak reaching to her feet, entered. She was tall and slight, with fair hair.

'I knew you would not mind. I wished to see you so!'

The woman offered her a seat by the fire. 'May I loosen your cloak? – the room is warm.'

'I wanted so to come and see you. You are the only person in the world who could help me! I know you are so large, and generous, and kind to other women!' She sat down. Tears stood in her large blue eyes: she was pulling off her little gloves unconsciously.

'You know Mr – ' (she mentioned the name of a well-known writer): 'I know you meet him often in your work. I want you to do something for me!'

The woman on the hearthrug looked down at her.

'I couldn't tell my father or my mother, or any one else; but I can tell you, though I know so little of you. You know, last summer he came and stayed with us a month. I saw a great deal of him. I don't know if he liked me; I know he liked my singing, and we rode together – I liked him more than any man I have ever seen. Oh, you know it isn't true that a woman can only like a man when he likes her; and I thought, perhaps, he liked me a little. Since we have been in town we have asked, but he has never come to see us. Perhaps people have been saying something to him about me. You know him, you are always meeting him, couldn't you say or do anything for me?' She looked up with her lips white and drawn. 'I feel sometimes as if I were going mad! Oh, it is so terrible to be a woman!' The woman looked down at her. 'Now I hear he likes another woman. I don't know who she is, but they say she is so clever, and writes. Oh, it is so terrible, I can't bear it.'

The woman leaned her elbow against the mantelpiece, and her face against her hand. She looked down into the fire. Then she turned and looked at the younger woman. 'Yes,' she said, 'it is a very terrible thing to be a woman.' She was silent. She said with some difficulty: 'Are you sure you love him? Are you sure it is not only the feeling a young girl has for an older man who is celebrated, and of whom every one is talking?'

'I have been nearly mad. I haven't slept for weeks!' She knit her little hands together, till the jewelled ring almost cut into the fingers. 'He is everything to me; there is nothing else in the world. You, who are so great, and strong, and clever, and who care only for your work, and for men as your friends, you cannot understand what it is when one person is everything to you, when there is nothing else in the world!'

'And what do you want me to do?'

'Oh, I don't know!' She looked up. 'A woman knows what she can do. Don't tell him that I love him.' She looked up again. 'Just say something to him. Oh, it's so terrible to be a woman; I can't do anything. You won't tell him exactly that I love him? That's the thing that makes a man hate a woman, if you tell it him plainly.'

'If I speak to him I must speak openly. He is my friend. I cannot fence with him. I have never fenced with him in my own affairs.' She moved as though she were going away from the fireplace, then she turned and said: 'Have you thought of what love is between a man and a woman when it means marriage? That long, long life together, day after day, stripped of all romance and distance, living face to face: seeing each other as a man sees his own soul? Do you realize that the end of marriage is to make the man and woman stronger than they were; and that if you cannot, when you are an old man and woman and sit by the fire, say, 'Life has been a braver and a freer thing for us, because we passed it hand in hand, than if we had passed through it alone,' it has failed? Do you care for him enough to live for him, not tomorrow, but when he is an old, faded man, and you an old, faded woman? Can you forgive him his sins and his weaknesses, when they hurt you most? If he were to lie a querulous invalid for twenty years, would you be able to fold him in your arms all that time, and comfort him, as a mother comforts her little child?' The woman drew her breath heavily.

'Oh, I love him absolutely! I would be glad to die,

if only I could once know that he loved me better than anything in the world!'

The woman stood looking down at her. 'Have you never thought of that other woman; whether *she* could not perhaps make his life as perfect as you?' she asked, slowly.

'Oh, no woman ever could be to him what I would be. I would live for him. He belongs to me.' She bent herself forward, not crying, but her shoulders moving. 'It is such a terrible thing to be a woman, to be able to do nothing and say nothing!'

The woman put her hand on her shoulder; the younger woman looked up into her face; then the elder turned away and stood looking into the fire. There was such quiet, you could hear the clock tick above the writing-table.

The woman said: 'There is one thing I can do for you. I do not know if it will be of any use – I will do it.' She turned away.

'Oh, you are so great and good, so beautiful, so different from other women, who are always thinking only of themselves! Thank you so much. I know I can trust you. I couldn't have told my mother, or any one but you.'

'Now you must go; I have my work to finish.'

The younger woman put her arms round her. 'Oh, you are so good and beautiful!'

The silk dress and the fur cloak rustled out of the room.

The woman who was left alone walked up and down, at last faster and faster, till the drops stood on her forehead. After a time she went up to the table: there was written illegibly in a man's hand on a fragment of manuscript paper: 'Can I come to see you this afternoon?' Near it was a closed and addressed envelope. She opened it. In it were written the words:

'Yes, please, come.'

She tore it across and wrote the words: 'No, I shall not be at liberty.'

She closed them in an envelope and addressed them. Then she rolled up the manuscript on the table and rang the bell. She gave it to the servant. 'Tell the boy to give this to his master, and say the article ends rather abruptly; they must state it is to be continued; I will finish it tomorrow. As he passes No. 20 let him leave this note there.'

The servant went out. She walked up and down with her hands folded above her head.

Two months after, the older woman stood before the fire. The door opened suddenly, and the younger woman came in.

'I had to come – I couldn't wait. You have heard, he was married this morning? Oh, do you think it is true? Do help me!' She put out her hands.

'Sit down. Yes, it is quite true.'

'Oh, it is so terrible, and I didn't know anything! Did you ever say anything to him?' She caught the woman's hands.

'I never saw him again after the day you were here – so I could not speak to him – but I did what I could.' She stood looking passively into the fire.

'And they say she is quite a child, only eighteen. They say he only saw her three times before he proposed to her. Do you think it is true?'

'Yes, it is quite true.'

'He can't love her. They say he's only marrying her for her rank and her money.'

The woman turned quickly. 'What right have you to say that? No one but me knows him. What need has he of any one's rank or wealth? He is greater than them all! Older women may have failed him; he has needed to turn to her beautiful, fresh young life to compensate him. She is a woman whom any man might have loved, so young and beautiful; her family are famed for their intellect. If he trains her, she may make him a better wife than any other woman would have done.'

'Oh, but I can't bear it – I can't bear it!' The younger woman sat down in the chair. 'She will be his wife, and have his children.'

'Yes.' The elder woman moved quickly. 'One wants to have the child, and lay its head on one's breast and feed it.' She moved quickly. 'It would not matter if another woman bore it, if one had it to take care of.' She moved restlessly.

'Oh, no, I couldn't bear it to be hers. When I think of her I feel as if I were dying; all my fingers turn cold; I feel dead. Oh, you were only his friend; you don't know!'

The older spoke softly and quickly. 'Don't you feel a little gentle to her when you think she's going to be his wife and the mother of his child? I would like to put my arms round her and touch her once, if she would let me. She is so beautiful, they say.'

'Oh, I could never bear to see her; it would kill me. And they are so happy together today! He is loving her so!'

'Don't you want him to be happy?' The older woman looked down at her. 'Have you *never* loved him, at all?'

The younger woman's face was covered with her hands. 'Oh, it's so terrible, so dark! and I shall go on living year after year, always in this awful pain! Oh, if I could only die!'

The older woman stood looking into the fire; then slowly and measuredly she said: 'There are times, in life, when everything seems dark, when the brain reels, and we cannot see that there is anything but death. But, if we wait long enough, after long, long years, calm comes. It may be we cannot say it was well; but we are contented, we accept the past. The struggle is ended. That day may come for you, perhaps sooner than you think.' She spoke slowly, and with difficulty.

'No, it can never come for me. If once I have loved a thing, I love it for ever. I can never forget.'

'Love is not the only end in life. There are other things to live for.'

'Oh yes, for you! To me love is everything!'

'Now, you must go, dear.'

The younger woman stood up. 'It has been such a comfort to talk to you. I think I should have killed myself if I had not come. You help me so. I shall always be grateful to you.'

The older woman took her hand.

'I want to ask something of you?'

'What is it?'

'I cannot quite explain to you. You will not understand. But there are times when something more terrible can come into a life than that it should lose what it loves. If you have had a dream of what life ought to be, and you try to make it real, and you fail; and something you have killed out in your heart for long years wakes up and cries, "Let each man play his own game, and care nothing for the hand of his fellow! Each man for himself. *So* the game must be played!" and you doubt all you have lived for, and the ground seems washing out under your feet —' She paused. 'Such a time has come to me now. If you would promise me that if ever another woman comes to seek your help, you will give it to her, and try to love her for my sake, I think it will help me. I think I should be able to keep my faith.'

'Oh, I will do anything you ask me to. You are so good and great.'

'Oh, good and great! – if you knew! Now go, dear.'

'I have not kept you from your work, have I?'

'No; I have not been working lately. Goodbye, dear.'

The younger woman went; and the elder knelt down by the chair, and wailed like a little child when you have struck it and it does not dare to cry loud.

A year after; it was early spring again.

The woman sat at her desk writing; behind her the fire burnt brightly. She was writing a leading article on the causes which in differing peoples lead to the adoption of Free Trade or Protectionist principles.

The woman wrote on quickly. After a while the servant entered and laid a pile of letters on the table. 'Tell the boy I shall have done in fifteen minutes.' She wrote on. Then she caught sight of the writing on one of the letters. She put down her pen, and opened it. It ran so:

Dear Friend, – I am writing to you, because I know you will rejoice to hear of my great happiness. Do you remember how you told me that day by the fire to *wait*, and after long, long years I should see that all was for the best? That time has come sooner than we hoped. Last week in Rome I was married to the best, noblest, most large-hearted of men. We are now in Florence together. You don't know how beautiful all life is to me. I know now that the old passion was only a girl's foolish dream. My husband is the first man I have ever truly loved. He loves me and understands me as no other man ever could. I am thankful that my dream was broken; God had better things in store for me. I don't hate that woman any more; I love every one! How are you, dear? We shall come and see you as soon as we arrive in England. I always think of you so happy in your great work and helping other people. I don't think *now* it is terrible to be a woman; it is lovely.

I hope you are enjoying this beautiful spring weather.

Yours always full of gratitude and love,

E –.

The woman read the letter: then she stood up and walked towards the fire. She did not re-read it, but stood with it open in her hand, looking down into the blaze. Her lips were drawn in at the corners. Presently she tore the letter up slowly, and watched the bits floating down one by one into the grate. Then she went back to her desk, and began to write, with her mouth still drawn in at the corners. After a while she laid her arm on the paper and her head on her arm, and seemed to go to sleep there.

Presently the servant knocked; the boy was waiting. 'Tell him to wait ten minutes more.' She took up her pen – 'The policy of the Australian Colonies in favour of Protection is easily understood – ' she waited – 'when one considers the fact – the fact – '; then she finished the article.

(*Cape Town, South Africa, 1892*)

10 Three Dreams in a Desert

Under a Mimosa Tree

As I travelled across an African plain the sun shone down hotly. Then I drew my horse up under a mimosa tree, and I took the saddle from him and left him to feed among the parched bushes. And all to right and to left stretched the brown earth. And I sat down under the tree, because the heat beat fiercely, and all along the horizon the air throbbed. And after a while a heavy drowsiness came over me, and I laid my head down against my saddle, and I fell asleep there. And, in my sleep, I had a curious dream.

I thought I stood on the border of a great desert, and the sand blew about everywhere. And I thought I saw two great figures like beasts of burden of the desert, and one lay upon the sand with its neck stretched out, and one stood by it. And I looked curiously at the one that lay upon the ground, for it had a great burden on its back, and the sand was thick about it, so that it seemed to have piled over it for centuries.

And I looked very curiously at it. And there stood one beside me watching. And I said to him, ‘What is this huge creature who lies here on the sand?’

And he said, 'This is woman; she that bears men in her body.'

And I said, 'Why does she lie here motionless with the sand piled round her?'

And he answered, 'Listen, I will tell you! Ages and ages long she has lain here, and the wind has blown over her. The oldest, oldest, oldest man living has never seen her move: the oldest, oldest book records that she lay here then, as she lies here now, with the sand about her. But listen! Older than the oldest book, older than the oldest recorded memory of man, on the Rocks of Language, on the hard-baked clay of Ancient Customs now crumbling to decay, are found the marks of her footsteps! Side by side with his who stands beside her you may trace them; and you know that she who now lies there once wandered free over the rocks with him.'

And I said, 'Why does she lie there now?'

And he said, 'I take it, ages ago the Age-of-dominion-of-muscular-force found her and when she stooped low to give suck to her young, and her back was broad, he put his burden of subjection on to it, and tied it on with the broad band of Inevitable Necessity. Then she looked at the earth and the sky, and knew there was no hope for her; and she lay down on the sand with the burden she could not loosen. Ever since she has lain there. And the ages have come, and the ages have gone, but the band of Inevitable Necessity has not been cut.'

And I looked and saw in her eyes the terrible patience of the centuries; the ground was wet with her tears, and her nostrils blew up the sand.

And I said, 'Has she ever tried to move?'

And he said, 'Sometimes a limb has quivered. But she is wise; she knows she cannot rise with the burden on her.'

And I said, 'Why does not he who stands by her leave her and go on?'

And he said, 'He cannot. Look – '

And I saw a broad band passing along the ground from one to the other, and it bound them together.

He said, 'While she lies there he must stand and look across the desert.'

And I said, 'Does he know why he cannot move?'

And he said, 'No.'

And I heard a sound of something cracking, and I looked, and I saw the band that bound the burden on to her back broken asunder; and the burden rolled on to the ground.

And I said, 'What is this?'

And he said, 'The Age-of-muscular-force is dead. The Age-of-nervous-force has killed him with the knife he holds in his hand; and silently and invisibly he has crept up to the woman, and with that knife of Mechanical Invention he has cut the band that bound the burden to her back. The Inevitable Necessity is broken. She might rise now.'

And I saw that she still lay motionless on the sand, with her eyes open and her neck stretched out. And she seemed to look for something on the far-off border of the desert that never came. And I wondered if she were awake or asleep. And as I looked her body quivered, and a light came into her eyes, like when a sunbeam breaks into a dark room.

I said, 'What is it?'

He whispered, 'Hush! the thought has come to her, "Might I not rise?"'

And I looked. And she raised her head from the sand, and I saw the dent where her neck had lain so long. And she looked at the earth, and she looked at the sky, and she looked at him who stood by her: but he looked out across the desert.

And I saw her body quiver; and she pressed her front knees to the earth, and veins stood out; and I cried, 'She is going to rise!'

But only her sides heaved, and she lay still where she was.

But her head she held up; she did not lay it down again. And he beside me said, 'She is very weak. See, her legs have been crushed under her so long.'

And I saw the creature struggle: and the drops stood out on her.

And I said, 'Surely he who stands beside her will help her?'

And he beside me answered, 'He cannot help her: *she must help herself.* Let her struggle till she is strong.'

And I cried, 'At least he will not hinder her! See, he moves farther from her, and tightens the cord between them, and he drags her down.'

And he answered, 'He does not understand. When she moves she draws the band that binds them, and hurts him, and he moves farther from her. The day will come when he will understand, and will know what she is doing. Let her once stagger on to her knees. In that day he will stand close to her, and look into her eyes with sympathy.'

And she stretched her neck, and the drops fell from her. And the creature rose an inch from the earth and sank back.

And I cried, 'Oh, she is too weak! she cannot walk! The long years have taken all her strength from her. Can she never move?'

And he answered me, 'See the light in her eyes!'

And slowly the creature staggered on to its knees.

And I awoke: and all to the east and to the west stretched the barren earth, with the dry bushes on it.

The ants ran up and down in the red sand, and the heat beat fiercely. I looked up through the thin branches of the tree at the blue sky overhead. I stretched myself, and I mused over the dream I had had. And I fell asleep again, with my head on my saddle. And in the fierce heat I had another dream.

I saw a desert and I saw a woman coming out of it. And she came to the bank of a dark river; and the bank was steep and high. And on it an old man met her, who had a long white beard; and a stick that curled was in his hand, and on it was written Reason. And he asked her what she wanted; and she said, 'I am woman; and I am seeking for the Land of Freedom.'

And he said, 'It is before you.'

And she said, 'I see nothing before me but a dark flowing river, and a bank steep and high, and cuttings here and there with heavy sand in them.'

And he said, 'And beyond that?'

She said, 'I see nothing, but sometimes, when I shade my eyes with my hand, I think I see on the further bank trees and hills, and the sun shining on them!'

He said, 'That is the Land of Freedom.'

She said, 'How am I to get there?'

He said, 'There is one way, and one only. Down the banks of Labour, through the water of Suffering. There is no other.'

She said, 'Is there no bridge?'

He answered, 'None.'

She said, 'Is the water deep?'

He said, 'Deep.'

She said, 'Is the floor worn?'

He said, 'It is. Your foot may slip at any time, and you may be lost.'

She said, 'Have any crossed already?'

He said, 'Some have *tried!*'

She said, 'Is there a track to show where the best fording is?'

He said, 'It has to be made.'

She shaded her eyes with her hand; and she said, 'I will go.'

And he said, 'You must take off the clothes you wore in the desert: they are dragged down by them who go into the water so clothed.'

And she threw from her gladly the mantle of Ancient-received-opinions she wore, for it was worn full of holes. And she took the girdle from her waist that she had treasured so long, and the moths flew out of it in a cloud. And he said, 'Take the shoes of dependence off your feet.'

And she stood there naked, but for one white garment that clung close to her.

And he said, 'That you may keep. So they wear clothes in the Land of Freedom. In the water it buoys; it always swims.'

And I saw on its breast was written Truth; and it was white; the sun had not often shone on it; the other clothes had covered it up. And he said, 'Take this stick; hold it fast. In that day when it slips from your hand you are lost. Put it down before you; feel your way: where it cannot find a bottom do not set your foot.'

And she said, 'I am ready; let me go.'

And he said, 'No – but stay; what is that – in your breast?'

She was silent.

He said, 'Open it, and let me see.'

And she opened it. And against her breast was a tiny thing, who drank from it, and the yellow curls above his forehead pressed against it; and his knees were drawn up to her, and he held her breast fast with his hands.

And Reason said, 'Who is he, and what is he doing here?'

And she said, 'See his little wings – '

And Reason said, 'Put him down.'

And she said, 'He is asleep, and he is drinking! I will carry him to the Land of Freedom. He has been a child so long, so long, I have carried him. In the Land of Freedom he will be a man. We will walk together there, and his great white wings will overshadow me. He has lisped one word only to me in the desert – "Passion!" I have dreamed he might learn to say "Friendship" in that land.'

And Reason said, 'Put him down!'

And she said, 'I will carry him so – with one arm, and with the other I will fight the water.'

He said, 'Lay him down on the ground. When you are in the water you will forget to fight, you will think only of him. Lay him down.' He said, 'He will not die. When he finds you have left him alone he will open his wings and fly. He will be in the Land of Freedom before you. Those who reach the Land of Freedom, the first hand they see stretching down the bank to help them shall be Love's. He will be a man then, not a child. In your breast he cannot thrive; put him down that he may grow.'

And she took her bosom from his mouth, and he bit her, so that the blood ran down on to the ground. And she laid him down on the earth; and she covered her wound. And she bent and stroked his wings. And I saw the hair on her forehead turned white as snow, and she had changed from youth to age.

And she stood far off on the bank of the river. And she said, 'For what do I go to this far land which no one has ever reached? *Oh, I am alone! I am utterly alone!*'

And Reason, that old man, said to her, 'Silence!

what do you hear?'

And she listened intently, and she said, 'I hear a sound of feet, a thousand times ten thousand and thousands of thousands, and they beat this way!'

He said, 'They are the feet of those that shall follow you. Lead on! make a track to the water's edge! Where you stand now, the ground will be beaten flat by ten thousand times ten thousand feet.' And he said, 'Have you seen the locusts, how they cross a stream? First one comes down to the water-edge, and it is swept away, and then another comes and then another, and then another, and at last with their bodies piled up a bridge is built and the rest pass over.'

She said, 'And, of those that come first some are swept away, and are heard of no more; their bodies do not even build the bridge?'

'And are swept away, and are heard of no more – and what of that?' he said.

'And what of that – ' she said.

'They make a track to the water's edge.'

'They make a track to the water's edge – .' And she said, 'Over that bridge which shall be built with our bodies, who will pass?'

He said, '*The entire human race.*'

And the woman grasped her staff.

And I saw her turn down that dark path to the river.

And I awoke; and all about me was the yellow afternoon light: the sinking sun lit up the fingers of the milkbushes; and my horse stood by me quietly feeding. And I turned on my side, and I watched the ants run by thousands in the red sand. I thought I would go on my way now – the afternoon was cooler. Then a drowsiness crept over me again, and I laid back my head and fell asleep.

And I dreamed a dream.

I dreamed I saw a land. And on the hills walked brave women and brave men, hand in hand. And they looked into each other's eyes, and they were not afraid.

And I saw the women also hold each other's hands.

And I said to him beside me, 'What place is this?'

And he said, 'This is heaven.'

And I said, 'Where is it?'

And he answered, 'On earth.'

And I said, 'When shall these things be?'

And he answered, 'In the future.'

And I awoke, and all about me was the sunset light; and on the low hills the sun lay, and a delicious coolness had crept over everything; and the ants were going slowly home. And I walked towards my horse, who stood quietly feeding. Then the sun passed down behind the hills; but I knew that the next day he would arise again.

(*Published in London, 1887*)

11 Eighteen Ninety-nine

'Thou fool, that which thou sowest is not quickened unless it die.'

1

It was a warm night: the stars shone down through the thick soft air of the northern Transvaal into the dark earth, where a little daub-and-wattle house of two rooms lay among the long, grassy slopes.

A light shone through the small window of the house, though it was past midnight. Presently the upper half of the door opened and then the lower, and the tall figure of a woman stepped out into the darkness. She closed the door behind her and walked towards the back of the house where a large round hut stood; beside it lay a pile of stumps and branches quite visible when once the eyes grew accustomed to the darkness. The woman stooped and broke off twigs till she had her apron full, and then returned slowly, and went into the house.

The room to which she returned was a small, bare room, with brown earthen walls and a mud floor; a naked deal table stood in the centre, and a few dark wooden chairs, home-made, with seats of undressed leather, stood round the walls. In the corner opposite the door was an open fireplace, and on the earthen hearth stood an iron three-foot, on which stood a large black kettle, under which coals were smouldering, though the night was hot and close. Against the wall on the left side of the room hung a gun-rack with three guns upon it, and below it a large hunting-watch hung from two nails by its silver chain.

In the corner by the fireplace was a little table with a coffee-pot upon it and a dish containing cups and saucers covered with water, and above it were a few shelves with crockery and a large Bible; but the dim light of the tallow candle which burnt on the table, with its wick of twisted rag, hardly made the corners visible. Beside the table sat a young woman, her head resting on her folded arms, the light of the tallow candle falling full on her head of pale flaxen hair, a little tumbled, and drawn behind into a large knot. The arms crossed on the table, from which the cotton sleeves had fallen back, were the full, rounded arms of one very young.

The older woman, who had just entered, walked to the fireplace, and kneeling down before it took from her apron the twigs and sticks she had gathered and heaped them under the kettle till a blaze sprang up which illumined the whole room. Then she rose up and sat down on a chair before the fire, but facing the table, with her hands crossed on her brown apron.

She was a woman of fifty, spare and broad-shouldered, with black hair, already slightly streaked with grey; from below high, arched eyebrows, and a high forehead, full dark eyes looked keenly, and a sharply cut aquiline nose gave strength to the face; but the mouth below was somewhat sensitive, and not over-full. She crossed and recrossed her knotted hands on her brown apron.

The woman at the table moaned and moved her head from side to side.

'What time is it?' she asked.

The older woman crossed the room to where the hunting-watch hung on the wall.

It showed a quarter past one, she said, and went back to her seat before the fire, and sat watching the figure beside the table, the firelight bathing her strong upright form and sharp aquiline profile.

Nearly fifty years before her parents had left the Cape Colony, and had set out on the long trek northward, and she, a young child, had been brought with them. She had no remembrance of the colonial home. Her first dim memories were of travelling in an ox-wagon; of dark nights when a fire was lighted in the open air, and people sat round it on the ground, and some faces seemed to stand out more than others in her memory which she thought must be those of her father and mother and of an old grandmother; she could remember lying awake in the back of the wagon while it was moving on, and the stars were shining down on her; and she had a vague memory of great wide plains with buck on them, which she thought must have been in the Free State. But the first thing which sprang out sharp and clear from the past was a day when she and another child, a little boy cousin of her own age, were playing among the bushes on the bank of a stream; she remembered how, suddenly, as they looked through the bushes, they saw black men leap out, and mount the ox-wagon outspanned under the trees; she remembered how they shouted and dragged people along, and stabbed them; she remembered how the blood gushed, and how they, the two young children among the bushes, lay flat on their stomachs and did not move or breathe, with that strange self-preserving instinct found in the young of animals or men who grow up in the open.

She remembered how black smoke came out at the back of the wagon and then red tongues of flame through the top; and even that some of the branches of the tree under which the wagon stood caught fire. She remembered later, when the black men had gone, and it was dark, that they were very hungry, and crept out to where the wagon had stood, and that they looked about on the ground for any scraps of food they might pick up, and that when they could not find any they cried. She remembered nothing clearly after that till some men with large beards and large hats rode up on horseback: it might have been next day or the day after. She remembered how they jumped off their horses and took them up in their arms, and how they cried; but that they, the children, did not cry, they only asked for food. She remembered how one man took a bit of thick, cold roosterkoek out of his pocket, and gave it to her, and how nice it tasted. And she remembered that the men took them up before them on their horses, and that one man tied her close to him with a large red handkerchief.

In the years that came she learnt to know that that which she remembered so clearly was the great and terrible day when, at Weenen, and in the country round, hundreds of women and children and youths and old men fell before the Zulus, and the assegais of Dingaan's braves drank blood.

She learnt that on that day all of her house and name, from the grandmother to the baby in arms, fell, and that she only and the boy cousin, who had hidden with her among the bushes, were left of all her kin in that northern world. She learnt, too, that the man who tied her to him with the red handkerchief took them back to his wagon, and that he and his wife adopted them, and brought them up among their own children.

She remembered, though less clearly than the day

of the fire, how a few years later they trekked away from Natal, and went through great mountain ranges, ranges in and near which lay those places the world was to know later as Laing's Nek, and Amajuba, and Ingogo; Elandslaagte, Nicholson's Nek, and Spionkop. She remembered how at last after many wanderings they settled down near the Witwatersrand, where game was plentiful and wild beasts were dangerous, but there were no natives, and they were far from the English rule.

There the two children grew up among the children of those who had adopted them, and were kindly treated by them as though they were their own; it yet was but natural that these two of the same name and blood should grow up with a peculiar tenderness for each other. And so it came to pass that when they were both eighteen years old they asked consent of the old people, who gave it gladly, that they should marry. For a time the young couple lived on in the house with the old, but after three years they gathered together all their few goods and in their wagon, with their guns and ammunition and a few sheep and cattle, they moved away northwards to found their own home.

For a time they travelled here and travelled there, but at last they settled on a spot where game was plentiful and the soil good, and there among the low undulating slopes, near the bank of a dry sloot, the young man built at last, with his own hands, a little house of two rooms.

On the long slope across the sloot before the house, he ploughed a piece of land and enclosed it, and he built kraals for his stock and so struck root in the land and wandered no more. Those were brave, glad, free days to the young couple. They lived largely on the game which the gun brought down, antelope and wildebeest that wandered even past the doors at night; and now and again a lion was killed: one no farther than the door of the round hut behind the house where the meat and the milk were stored, and two were killed at the kraals. Sometimes, too, traders came with their wagons and in exchange for skins and fine horns sold sugar and coffee and print and tan-cord, and such things as the little household had need of. The lands yielded richly to them, in maize, and pumpkins, and sweet cane, and melons; and they had nothing to wish for. Then in time three little sons were born to them, who grew as strong and vigorous in the free life of the open veld as the young lions in the long grass and scrub near the river four miles away. Those were joyous, free years for the man and woman, in which disease, and carking care, and anxiety played no part.

Then came a day when their eldest son was ten years old, and the father went out a-hunting with his Kaffir servants: in the evening they brought him home with a wound eight inches long in his side where a lioness had torn him; they brought back her skin also, as he had shot her at last in the hand-to-throat struggle. He lingered for three days and then died. His wife buried him on the low slope to the left of the house; she and her Kaffir servants alone made the grave and put him in it, for there were no white men near. Then she and her sons lived on there; a new root driven deep into the soil and binding them to it through the grave on the hillside. She hung her husband's large hunting-watch up on the wall, and put three of his guns over it on the rack, and the gun he had in his hand when he met his death she took down and polished up every day; but one gun she always kept loaded at the head of her bed in the inner room. She counted the stock every night and saw that the Kaffirs ploughed the lands, and she saw to the planting and watering of them herself.

Often as the years passed men of the countryside, and even from far off, heard of the young handsome widow who lived alone with her children and saw to her own stock and lands; and they came a-courting. But many of them were afraid to say anything when once they had come, and those who had spoken to her, when once she had answered them, never came again. About this time too the countryside began to fill in; and people came and settled as near as eight and ten miles away; and as people increased the game began to vanish, and with the game the lions, so that the one her husband killed was almost the last ever seen there. But there was still game enough for food, and when her eldest son was twelve years old, and she gave him his father's smallest gun to go out hunting with, he returned home almost every day with meat enough for the household tied behind his saddle. And as time passed she came also to be known through the countryside as a 'wise woman'. People came to her to ask advice about their illnesses, or to ask her to dress old wounds that would not heal; and when they questioned her whether she thought the rains would be early, or the game plentiful that year, she was nearly always right. So they called her a 'wise woman' because neither she nor they knew any word in that up-country speech of theirs for the thing called 'genius'. So all things went well till the eldest son was eighteen, and the dark beard was beginning to sprout on his face, and his mother began to think that soon there might be a daughter in the house, for on Saturday evenings, when his work was done, he put on his best clothes and rode off to the next farm eight miles away, where was a young daughter. His mother always saw that he had a freshly ironed shirt waiting for him on his bed, when he came home from the kraals on Saturday nights, and she made plans as to how they would build on two rooms for the new daughter. At this time he was training young horses to have them ready to sell when the traders came round: he was a fine rider and it was always his work. One afternoon he mounted a young horse before the door and it bucked and threw him. He had often fallen before, but this time his neck was broken. He lay dead with his head two feet from his mother's doorstep. They took up his tall, strong body and the next day the neighbours came from the next farm and they buried him beside his father, on the hillside, and another root was struck into the soil. Then the three who were left in the little farmhouse lived and worked on as before, for a year and more.

Then a small native war broke out, and the young burghers of the district were called out to help. The second son was very young, but he was the best shot in the district, so he went away with the others. Three months after the men came back, but among the few who did not return was her son. On a hot sunny afternoon, walking through a mealie field which they thought was deserted and where the dried yellow stalks stood thick, an assegai thrown from an unseen hand found him, and he fell there. His comrades took him and buried him under a large thorn tree, and scraped the earth smooth over him, that his grave might not be found by others. So he was not laid on the rise to the left of the house with his kindred, but his mother's heart went often to that thorn tree in the far north. And now again there were only two in the little mud house; as there had been years before when the young man and wife first settled there. She and her young lad were always together night and day, and did all that they did together, as though they were mother and daughter. He was a fair lad, tall and gentle as his father had been before him, not huge and dark as his two elder brothers; but he seemed to ripen towards manhood early. When he was only sixteen the thick white down was already gathering heavy on his upper lip; his mother watched him narrowly, and had many thoughts in her heart. One evening as they sat twisting wicks for the candles together, she said to him, 'You will be eighteen on your next birthday, my son, that was your father's age when he married me.' He said, 'Yes,' and they spoke no more then. But later in the evening when they sat before the door she said to him: 'We are very lonely here. I often long to hear the feet of a little child about the house, and to see one with your father's blood in it play before the door as you and your brothers played. Have you ever thought that you are the last of your father's name and blood left here in the north; that if you died there would be none left?' He said he had thought of it. Then she told him she thought it would be well if he went away, to the part of the country where the people lived who had brought her up: several of the sons and daughters who had grown up with her had now grown up children. He might go down and from among them seek out a young girl whom he liked and who liked him; and if he found her, bring her back as a wife. The lad thought very well of his mother's plan. And when three months were passed, and the ploughing season was over, he rode away one day, on the best black horse they had, his Kaffir boy riding behind him on another, and his mother stood at the gable watching them ride away. For three months she heard nothing of him, for trains were not in those days, and letters came rarely and by chance, and neither he nor she could read or write. One afternoon she stood at the gable end as she always stood when her work was done, looking out along the road that came over the rise, and she saw a large tent-wagon coming along it, and her son walking beside it. She walked to meet it. When she had greeted her son and climbed into the wagon she found there a girl of fifteen with pale flaxen hair and large blue eyes whom he had brought home as his wife. Her father had given her the wagon and oxen as her wedding portion. The older woman's heart wrapped itself about the girl as though she had been the daughter she had dreamed to bear of her own body, and had never borne.

The three lived joyfully at the little house as though they were one person. The young wife had been accustomed to live in a larger house, and down south, where they had things they had not here. She had been to school, and learned to read and write, and she could even talk a little English; but she longed for none of the things which she had had; the little brown house was home enough for her.

After a year a child came, but, whether it were that the mother was too young, it only opened its eyes for an hour on the world and closed them again. The young mother wept bitterly, but her husband folded his arms about her, and the mother comforted both. 'You are young, my children, but we shall yet hear the sound of children's voices in the house,' she said; and after a little while the young mother was well again and things went on peacefully as before in the little home.

But in the land things were not going on peacefully. That was the time that the flag to escape from which the people had left their old homes in the colony, and had again left Natal when it followed them there, and had chosen to face the spear of the savage, and the conflict with wild beasts, and death by hunger and thirst in the wilderness rather than live under, had by force and fraud unfurled itself over them again. For the moment a great sullen silence brooded over the land. The people, slow of thought, slow of speech, determined in action, and unforgetting, sat still and waited. It was like the silence that rests over the land before an up-country thunderstorm breaks.

Then words came, 'They have not even given us the free government they promised' – then acts – the people rose. Even in that remote countryside the men began to mount their horses, and with their guns ride away to help. In the little mud house the young wife wept much when he said that he too was going. But when his mother helped him pack his saddle-bags she helped too; and on the day when the men from the next farm went, he rode away also with his gun by his side.

No direct news of the one they had sent away came to the waiting women at the farmhouse; then came fleet reports of the victories of Ingogo and Amajuba. Then came an afternoon after he had been gone two months. They had both been to the gable end to look out at the road, as they did continually amid their work, and they had just come in to drink their afternoon coffee when the Kaffir maid ran in to say she saw someone coming along the road who looked like her master. The women ran out. It was the white horse on which he had ridden away, but they almost doubted if it were he. He rode bending on his saddle, with his chin on his breast and his arm hanging at his side. At first they thought he had been wounded, but when they had helped him from his horse and brought him into the house they found it was only a deadly fever which was upon him. He had crept home to them by small stages. Hardly had he any spirit left to tell them of Ingogo, Laing's Nek, and Amajuba. For fourteen days he grew worse and on the fifteenth day he died. And the two women buried him where the rest of his kin lay on the hillside.

And so it came to pass that on that warm starlight night the two women were alone in the little mud house with the stillness of the veld about them; even their Kaffir servants asleep in their huts beyond the kraals; and the very sheep lying silent in the starlight. They two were alone in the little house, but they knew that before morning they would not be alone, they were awaiting the coming of the dead man's child.

The young woman with her head on the table groaned. 'If only my husband were here still,' she wailed. The old woman rose and stood beside her, passing her hard, work-worn hand gently over her shoulder as if she were a little child. At last she induced her to go and lie down in the inner room. When she had grown quieter and seemed to have fallen into a light sleep the old woman came to the front room again. It was almost two o'clock and the fire had burned low under the large kettle. She scraped the coals together and went out of the front door to fetch more wood, and closed the door behind her. The night air struck cool and fresh upon her face after the close air of the house, the stars seemed to be growing lighter as the night advanced, they shot down their light as from a million polished steel points. She walked to the back of the house where, beyond the round hut that served as a store-room, the woodpile lay. She bent down gathering sticks and chips till her apron was full, then slowly she raised herself and stood still. She looked upwards. It was a wonderful night. The white band of the Milky Way crossed the sky overhead, and from every side stars threw down their light, sharp as barbed spears, from the velvety blue-black of the sky. The woman raised her hand to her forehead as if pushing the hair farther off it, and stood motionless, looking up. After a long time she dropped her hand and began walking slowly towards the house. Yet once or twice on the way she paused and stood looking up. When she went into the house the woman in the inner room was again moving and moaning. She laid the sticks down before the fire and went into the next room. She bent down over the bed where the younger woman lay, and put her hand upon her. 'My daughter,' she said slowly, 'be comforted. A wonderful thing has happened to me. As I stood out in the starlight it was as though a voice came down to me and spoke. The child which will be born of you tonight will be a man-child and he will live to do great things for his land and for his people.'

Before morning there was the sound of a little wail in the mud house: and the child who was to do great things for his land and for his people was born.

2

Six years passed; and all was as it had been at the little house among the slopes. Only a new piece of land had been ploughed up and added to the land before the house, so that the ploughed land now almost reached to the ridge.

The young mother had grown stouter, and lost her pink and white; she had become a working woman, but she still had the large knot of flaxen hair behind her head and the large wondering eyes. She had many suitors in those six years, but she sent them all away. She said the old woman looked after the farm as well as any man might, and her son would be grown up by and by. The grandmother's hair was a little more streaked with grey, but it was as thick as ever, and her shoulders as upright; only some of her front teeth had fallen out, which made her lips close more softly.

The great change was that wherever the women went there was the flaxen-haired child to walk beside them holding on to their skirts or clasping their hands.

The neighbours said they were ruining the child: they let his hair grow long, like a girl's, because it curled; and they never let him wear velskoens like other children but always shop boots; and his mother sat up at night to iron his pinafores as if the next day were always a Sunday.

But the women cared nothing for what was said; to them he was not as any other child. He asked them strange questions they could not answer, and he never troubled them by wishing to go and play with the little Kaffirs as other children trouble. When neighbours came over and brought their children with them he ran away and hid in the sloot to play by himself till they were gone. No, he was not like other children!

When the women went to lie down on hot days after dinner sometimes, he would say that he did not want to sleep; but he would not run about and make a noise like other children – he would go and sit outside in the shade of the house, on the front door-step, quite still, with his little hands resting on his knees, and stare far away at the ploughed lands on the slope, or the shadows nearer; the women would open the bedroom window, and peep out to look at him as he sat there.

The child loved his mother and followed her about to the milk house, and to the kraals; but he loved his grandmother best.

She told him stories.

When she went to the lands to see how the Kaffirs

were ploughing he would run at her side holding her dress; when they had gone a short way he would tug gently at it and say, 'Grandmother, tell me things!'

And long before day broke, when it was yet quite dark, he would often creep from the bed where he slept with his mother into his grandmother's bed in the corner; he would put his arms round her neck and stroke her face till she woke, and then whisper softly, 'Tell me stories!' and she would tell them to him in a low voice not to wake the mother, till the cock crowed and it was time to get up and light the candle and the fire.

But what he liked best of all were the hot, still summer nights, when the women put their chairs before the door because it was too warm to go to sleep; and he would sit on the stofie at his grandmother's feet and lean his head against her knees, and she would tell him on and on of the things he liked to hear; and he would watch the stars as they slowly set along the ridge, or the moonlight, casting bright-edged shadows from the gable as she talked. Often after the mother had got sleepy and gone in to bed the two sat there together.

The stories she told him were always true stories of the things she had seen or of things she had heard. Sometimes they were stories of her own childhood: of the day when she and his grandfather hid among the bushes, and saw the wagon burnt; sometimes they were of the long trek from Natal to the Transvaal; sometimes of the things which happened to her and his grandfather when first they came to that spot among the ridges, of how there was no house there nor lands, only two bare grassy slopes when they outspanned their wagon there the first night; she told of a lion she once found when she opened the door in the morning, sitting, with paws crossed, upon the threshold, and how the grandfather jumped out of bed and reopened the door two inches, and shot it through the opening; the skin was kept in the round storehouse still, very old and mangy.

Sometimes she told him of the two uncles who were dead, and of his own father, and of all they had been and done. But sometimes she told him of things much farther off: of the old colony where she had been born, but which she could not remember, and of the things which happened there in the old days. She told him of how the British had taken the Cape over, and of how the English had hanged their men at the Slagtersnek for resisting the English government, and of how the friends and relations had been made to stand round to see them hanged whether they would or no, and of how the scaffold broke down as they were being hanged, and the people looking on cried aloud, 'It is the finger of God! They are saved!' but how the British hanged them up again. She told him of the great trek in which her parents had taken part to escape from under the British flag; of the great battles with Mzilikazi; and of the murder of Retief and his men by Dingaan, and of Dingaan's Day. She told him how the British government followed them into Natal, and of how they trekked north and east to escape from it again; and she told him of the later things, of the fight at Laing's Nek, and Ingogo, and Amajuba, where his father had been. Always she told the same story in exactly the same words over and over again, till the child knew them all by heart, and would ask for this and then that.

The story he loved best, and asked for more often than all the others, made his grandmother wonder, because it did not seem to her the story a child would best like; it was not a story of lion-hunting, or wars, or adventures. Continually when she asked what she should tell him, he said, 'About the mountains!'

It was the story of how the Boer women in Natal when the English commissioner came to annex their country, collected to meet him and pointing toward the Drakensberg Mountains said, 'We go across those mountains to freedom or to death!'

More than once, when she was telling him the story, she saw him stretch out his little arm and raise his hand, as though he were speaking.

One evening as he and his mother were coming home from the milking kraals, and it was getting dark, and he was very tired, having romped about shouting among the young calves and kids all the evening, he held her hand tightly.

'Mother,' he said suddenly, 'when I am grown up, I am going to Natal.'

'Why, my child?' she asked him; 'there are none of our family living there now.'

He waited a little, then said, very slowly, 'I am going to go and try to get our land back!'

His mother started; if there were one thing she was more firmly resolved on in her own mind than any other it was that he should never go to the wars. She began to talk quickly of the old white cow who had kicked the pail over as she was milked, and when she got to the house she did not even mention to the grandmother what had happened; it seemed better to forget.

One night in the rainy season when it was damp and chilly they sat round the large fireplace in the front room.

Outside the rain was pouring in torrents and you could hear the water rushing in the great dry sloot before the door. His grandmother, to amuse him, had sprung some dried mealies in the great black pot and sprinkled them with sugar, and now he sat on the stofie at her feet with a large lump of the sticky sweetmeat in his hand, watching the fire. His grandmother from above him was watching it also, and his mother in her elbow-chair on the other side of the fire had her eyes half closed and was nodding already with the warmth of the room and her long day's work. The child sat so quiet, the hand with the lump of sweetmeat resting on his knee, that his grandmother thought he had gone to sleep too. Suddenly he said without looking up, 'Grandmother?'

'Yes.'

He waited rather a long time, then said slowly, 'Grandmother, did God make the English too?'

She also waited for a while, then she said, 'Yes, my child; He made all things.'

They were silent again, and there was no sound but of the rain falling and the fire cracking and the sloot rushing outside. Then he drew his head backwards on to his grandmother's knee and looking up into her face, said, 'But, grandmother, why did He make them?'

Then she too was silent for a long time. 'My child,' at last she said, 'we cannot judge the ways of the Almighty. He does that which seems good in His own eyes.'

The child sat up and looked back at the fire. Slowly he tapped his knee with the lump of sweetmeat once or twice; then he began to munch it; and soon the mother started wide awake and said it was time for all to go to bed.

The next morning his grandmother sat on the front doorstep cutting beans in an iron basin; he sat beside her on the step pretending to cut too, with a short, broken knife. Presently he left off and rested his hands on his knees, looking away at the hedge beyond, with his small forehead knit tight between the eyes.

'Grandmother,' he said suddenly, in a small, almost shrill voice, 'do the English want *all* the lands of *all* the people?'

The handle of his grandmother's knife as she cut clinked against the iron side of the basin. 'All they can get,' she said.

After a while he made a little movement almost like a sigh, and took up his little knife again and went on cutting.

Some time after that, when a trader came by, his grandmother bought him a spelling-book and a slate and pencils, and his mother began to teach him to read and write. When she had taught him for a year he knew all she did. Sometimes when she was setting him a copy and left a letter out in a word, he would quietly take the pencil when she set it down and put the letter in, not with any idea of correcting her, but simply because it must be there.

Often at night when the child had gone to bed early, tired out with his long day's play, and the two women were left in the front room with the tallow candle burning on the table between them, then they talked of his future.

Ever since he had been born everything they had earned had been put away in the wagon chest under the grandmother's bed. When the traders with their wagons came round the women bought nothing except a few groceries and clothes for the child; even before they bought a yard of cotton print for a new apron they talked long and solemnly as to whether the old one might not be made to do by repatching; and they mixed much more dry pumpkin and corn with their coffee than before he was born. It was to earn more money that the large new piece of land had been added to the lands before the house.

They were going to have him educated. First he

was to be taught all they could at home, then to be sent away to a great school in the old colony, and then he was to go over the sea to Europe and come back an advocate or a doctor or a parson. The grandmother had made a long journey to the next town, to find out from the minister just how much it would cost to do it all.

In the evenings when they sat talking it over the mother generally inclined to his becoming a parson. She never told the grandmother why, but the real reason was because parsons do not go to the wars. The grandmother generally favoured his becoming an advocate, because he might become a judge. Sometimes they sat discussing these matters till the candle almost burnt out.

'Perhaps, one day,' the mother would at last say, 'he may yet become president!'

Then the grandmother would slowly refold her hands across her apron and say softly, 'Who knows? – who knows?'

Often they would get the box out from under the bed (looking carefully across to the corner to see he was fast asleep) and would count out all the money, though each knew to a farthing how much was there; then they would make it into little heaps, so much for this, so much for that, and then they would count on their fingers how many good seasons it would take to make the rest, and how old he would be.

When he was eight and had learnt all his mother could teach him, they sent him to school every day on an adjoining farm six miles off, where the people had a schoolmaster. Every day he rode over on the great white horse his father went to the wars with; his mother was afraid to let him ride alone at first, but his grandmother said he must learn to do everything alone. At four o'clock when he came back one or other of the women was always looking out to see the little figure on the tall horse coming over the ridge.

When he was eleven they gave him his father's smallest gun; and one day not long after he came back with his first small buck. His mother had the skin dressed and bound with red, and she laid it as a mat under the table, and even the horns she did not throw away, and saved them in the round house, because it was his first.

When he was fourteen the schoolmaster said he could teach him no more; that he ought to go to some larger school where they taught Latin and other difficult things; they had not yet money enough and he was not quite old enough to go to the old colony, so they sent him first to the highveld, where his mother's relations lived and where there were good schools, where they taught the difficult things; he could live with his mother's relations and come back once a year for the holidays.

They were great times when he came.

His mother made him koekies and sosaties, and nice things every day; and he used to sit on the stofie at her feet and let her play with his hair like when he was quite small. With his grandmother he talked. He tried to explain to her all he was learning, and he read the English newspapers to her (she could neither read in English nor Dutch), translating them. Most of all she liked his atlas. They would sometimes sit over it for half an hour in the evening tracing the different lands and talking of them. On the warm nights he used to sit outside on the stofie at her feet with his head against her knee, and they used to discuss things that were happening in other lands and in South Africa; and sometimes they sat there quite still together.

It was now he who had the most stories to tell; he

had seen Krugersdorp, and Johannesburg, and Pretoria; he knew the world; he was at Krugersdorp when Dr Jameson made his raid. Sometimes he sat for an hour, telling her of things, and she sat quietly listening.

When he was seventeen, nearly eighteen, there was money enough in the box to pay for his going to the colony and then to Europe; and he came home to spend a few months with them before he went.

He was very handsome now; not tall, and very slight, but with fair hair that curled close to his head, and white hands like a townsman. All the girls in the countryside were in love with him. They all wished he would come and see them. But he seldom rode from home except to go to the next farm where he had been at school. There lived little Aletta, who was the daughter of the woman his uncle had loved before he went to the Kaffir war and got killed. She was only fifteen years old, but they had always been great friends. She netted him a purse of green silk. He said he would take it with him to Europe, and would show it her when he came back and was an advocate; and he gave her a book with her name written in it, which she was to show to him.

These were the days when the land was full of talk; it was said the English were landing troops in South Africa, and wanted to have war. Often the neighbours from the nearest farms would come to talk about it (there were more farms now, the country was filling in, and the nearest railway station was only a day's journey off), and they discussed matters. Some said they thought there would be war; others again laughed, and said it would be only Jameson and his white flag again. But the grandmother shook her head, and if they asked her, 'Why,' she said, 'it will not be the war of a week, nor of a month; if it comes it will be the war of years,' but she would say nothing more.

Yet sometimes when she and her grandson were walking along together in the lands she would talk.

Once she said: 'It is as if a great heavy cloud hung just above my head, as though I wished to press it back with my hands and could not. It will be a great war – a great war. Perhaps the English government will take the land for a time, but they will not keep it. The gold they have fought for will divide them, till they slay one another over it.'

Another day she said: 'This land will be a great land one day with one people from the sea to the north – but we shall not live to see it.'

He said to her: 'But how can that be when we are all of different races?'

She said: 'The land will make us one. Were not our fathers of more than one race?'

Another day, when she and he were sitting by the table after dinner, she pointed to a sheet of exercise paper, on which he had been working out a problem and which was covered with algebraical symbols, and said, 'In fifteen years' time the government of England will not have one piece of land in all South Africa as large as that sheet of paper.'

One night when the milking had been late and she and he were walking down together from the kraals in the starlight she said to him: 'If this war comes let no man go to it lightly, thinking he will surely return home, nor let him go expecting victory on the next day. It will come at last, but not at first. Sometimes,' she said, 'I wake at night and it is as though the whole house were filled with smoke – and I have to get up and go outside to breathe. It is as though I saw my whole land blackened and desolate. But when I look up it is as though a voice cried out to me, "Have no fear!"'

They were getting his things ready for him to go away after Christmas. His mother was making him shirts and his grandmother was having a kaross of jackals' skins made that he might take it with him to Europe where it was so cold. But his mother noticed that whenever the grandmother was in the room with him and he was not looking at her, her eyes were always curiously fixed on him as though they were questioning something. The hair was growing white and a little thin over her temples now, but her eyes were as bright as ever, and she could do a day's work with any man.

One day when the youth was at the kraals helping the Kaffir boys to mend a wall, and the mother was kneading bread in the front room, and the grandmother washing up the breakfast things, the son of the field cornet came riding over from his father's farm, which was about twelve miles off. He stopped at the kraal and Jan and he stood talking for some time, then they walked down to the farmhouse, the Kaffir boy leading the horse behind them. Jan stopped at the round store, but the field cornet's son went to the front door. The grandmother asked him in, and handed him some coffee, and the mother, her hands still in the dough, asked him how things were going at his father's farm, and if his mother's young turkeys had come out well, and she asked if he had met Jan at the kraals. He answered the questions slowly, and sipped his coffee. Then he put the cup down on the table; and said suddenly in the same measured voice, staring at the wall in front of him, that war had broken out, and his father had sent him round to call out all fighting burghers.

The mother took her hands out of the dough and stood upright beside the trough as though paralysed. Then she cried in a high, hard voice, unlike her own,

'Yes, but Jan cannot go! He is hardly eighteen! He's got to go and be educated in other lands! You can't take the only son of a widow!'

'Aunt,' said the young man slowly, 'no one will make him go.'

The grandmother stood resting the knuckles of both hands on the table, her eyes fixed on the young man. 'He shall decide himself,' she said.

The mother wiped her hands from the dough and rushed past them and out at the door; the grandmother followed slowly.

They found him in the shade at the back of the house, sitting on a stump; he was cleaning the belt of his new Mauser which lay across his knees.

'Jan,' his mother cried, grasping his shoulder, 'you are not going away? You can't go! You must stay. You can go by Delagoa Bay if there is fighting on the other side! There is plenty of money!'

He looked softly up into her face with his blue eyes. 'We have all to be at the field cornet's at nine o'clock tomorrow morning,' he said. She wept aloud and argued.

His grandmother turned slowly without speaking, and went back into the house. When she had given the field cornet's son another cup of coffee, and shaken hands with him, she went into the bedroom and opened the box in which her grandson's clothes were kept, to see which things he should take with him. After a time the mother came back too. He had kissed her and talked to her until she too had at last said it was right he should go.

All day they were busy. His mother baked him biscuits to take in his bag, and his grandmother made a belt of two strips of leather; she sewed them together herself and put a few sovereigns between the stitchings. She said some of his comrades might need the money if he did not.

The next morning early he was ready. There were two saddle-bags tied to his saddle and before it was strapped the kaross his grandmother had made; she said it would be useful when he had to sleep on damp ground. When he had greeted them, he rode away towards the rise: and the women stood at the gable of the house to watch him.

When he had gone a little way he turned in his saddle, and they could see he was smiling; he took off his hat and waved it in the air; the early morning sunshine made his hair as yellow as the tassels that hang from the head of ripening mealies. His mother covered her face with the sides of her kappie and wept aloud; but the grandmother shaded her eyes with both her hands and stood watching him till the figure passed out of sight over the ridge; and when it was gone and the mother returned to the house crying, she still stood watching the line against the sky.

The two women were very quiet during the next days, they worked hard, and seldom spoke. After eight days there came a long letter from him (there was now a post once a week from the station to the field cornet's). He said he was well and in very good spirits. He had been to Krugersdorp, and Johannesburg, and Pretoria; all the family living there were well and sent greetings. He had joined a corps that was leaving for the front the next day. He sent also a long message to Aletta, asking them to tell her he was sorry to go away without saying goodbye; and he told his mother how good the biscuits and biltong were she had put into his saddle-bag; and he sent her a piece of vierkleur ribbon in the letter, to wear on her breast.

The women talked a great deal for a day or two after this letter came. Eight days after there was a short note from him, written in pencil in the train on his way to the front. He said all was going well, and if he did not write soon they were not to be anxious; he would write as often as he could.

For some days the women discussed that note too.

Then came two weeks without a letter, the two women became very silent. Every day they sent the Kaffir boy over to the field cornet's, even on the days when there was no post, to hear if there was any news.

Many reports were flying about the countryside. Some said that an English armoured train had been taken on the western border; that there had been fighting at Albertina, and in Natal. But nothing seemed quite certain.

Another week passed. . . Then the two women became very quiet.

The grandmother, when she saw her daughter-in-law left the food untouched on her plate, said there was no need to be anxious; men at the front could not always find paper and pencils to write with and might be far from any post office. Yet night after night she herself would rise from her bed saying she felt the house close, and go and walk up and down outside.

Then one day suddenly all their servants left them except one Kaffir and his wife, whom they had had for years, and the servants from the farms about went also, which was a sign there had been news of much fighting; for the Kaffirs hear things long before the white man knows them.

Three days after, as the women were clearing off the breakfast things, the youngest son of the field cornet, who was only fifteen and had not gone to the war with the others, rode up. He hitched his horse to the post, and came towards the door. The mother stepped forward to meet him and shook hands in the doorway.

'I suppose you have come for the carrot seed I promised your mother? I was not able to send it, as our servants ran away,' she said, as she shook his hand. 'There isn't a letter from Jan, is there?' The lad said no, there was no letter from him, and shook hands with the grandmother. He stood by the table instead of sitting down.

The mother turned to the fireplace to get coals to put under the coffee to rewarm it; but the grandmother stood leaning forward with her eyes fixed on him across the table. He felt uneasily in his breast pocket.

'Is there no news?' the mother said without looking round, as she bent over the fire.

'Yes, there is news, aunt.'

She rose quickly and turned towards him, putting down the brazier on the table. He took a letter out of his breast pocket. 'Aunt, my father said I must bring this to you. It came inside one to him and they asked him to send one of us over with it.'

The mother took the letter; she held it, examining the address.

'It looks to me like the writing of Sister Annie's Paul,' she said. 'Perhaps there is news of Jan in it' – she turned to them with a half-nervous smile – 'they were always such friends.'

'All is as God wills, aunt,' the young man said, looking down fixedly at the top of his riding-whip.

But the grandmother leaned forward motionless, watching her daughter-in-law as she opened the letter.

She began to read to herself, her lips moving slowly as she deciphered it word by word.

Then a piercing cry rang through the roof of the little mud farmhouse.

'He is dead! My boy is dead!'

She flung the letter on the table and ran out at the front door.

Far out across the quiet ploughed lands and over the veld to where the kraals lay the cry rang. The Kaffir woman who sat outside her hut beyond the kraals nursing her baby heard it and came down with her child across her hip to see what was the matter. At the side of the round house she stood motionless and open-mouthed, watching the woman, who paced up and down behind the house with her apron thrown over her head and her hands folded above it, crying aloud.

In the front room the grandmother, who had not spoken since he came, took up the letter and put it in the lad's hands. 'Read,' she whispered.

And slowly the lad spelled it out.

My Dear Aunt,

I hope this letter finds you well. The Commandant has asked me to write it.

We had a great fight four days ago, and Jan is dead. The Commandant says I must tell you how it happened. Aunt, there were five of us first in a position on that koppie, but two got killed, and then there was only three of us – Jan, and I, and Uncle Peter's Frikkie. Aunt, the khakis were coming on all round just like locusts, and the bullets were coming just like hail. It was bare on that side of the koppie where we were, but we had plenty of cartridges. We three took up a position where there were some small stones and we fought, Aunt; we had to. One bullet took off the top of my ear, and Jan got two bullets, one through the flesh in the left leg and one through his arm, but he could still fire his gun. Then we three meant to go to the top of the koppie, but a bullet took Jan right through his chest. We knew he couldn't go any farther. The khakis were right at the foot of the koppie just coming up. He told us to lay him down, Aunt. We said we would stay by him, but he said we must go. I put my jacket under his head and Frikkie put his over his feet. We threw his gun far away from him that they might see how it was with him. He said he hadn't much pain, Aunt. He was full of blood from his arm, but there wasn't much from his chest, only a little out of the corners of his mouth. He said we must make haste or the khakis would catch us; he said he wasn't afraid to be left there.

Aunt, when we got to the top, it was all full of khakis like the sea on the other side, all among the koppies and on our koppie too. We were surrounded, Aunt; the last I saw of Frikkie he was sitting on a stone with the blood running down his face, but he got under a rock and hid there; some of our men found him next morning and brought him to camp. Aunt, there was a khaki's horse standing just below where I was, with no one on it. I jumped on and rode. The bullets went this way and the bullets went that, but I rode! Aunt, the khakis were sometimes as near me as that tent-pole, only the grace of God saved me. It was dark in the night when I got back to where our people were, because I had to go round all the koppies to get away from the khakis.

Aunt, the next day we went to look for him. We found him where we left him; but he was turned over on to his face; they had taken all his things, his belt and his watch, and the puggaree from his hat, even his boots. The little green silk purse he used to carry we found on the ground by him, but nothing in it. I will send it back to you whenever I get an opportunity.

Aunt, when we turned him over on his back there were four bayonet stabs in his body. The doctor says it was only the first three while he was alive; the last one was through the heart and killed him at once.

We gave him a Christian burial, Aunt; we took him to the camp.

The Commandant was there, and all of the family who are with the Commando were there, and they all said they hoped God would comfort you. . .

The old woman leaned forward and grasped the boy's arm. 'Read it over again,' she said, 'from where they found him.' He turned back and re-read slowly. She gazed at the page as though she were reading also. Then, suddenly, she slipped out at the front door.

At the back of the house she found her daughter-in-law still walking up and down, and the Kaffir woman with a red handerchief bound round her head and the child sitting across her hip, sucking from her long, pendulous breast, looking on.

The old woman walked up to her daughter-in-law and grasped her firmly by the arm.

'He's dead! You know, my boy's dead!' she cried, drawing the apron down with her right hand and disclosing her swollen and bleared face. 'Oh, his beautiful hair – Oh, his beautiful hair!'

The old woman held her arm tighter with both hands; the younger opened her half-closed eyes, and looked into the keen, clear eyes fixed on hers, and stood arrested.

The old woman drew her face closer to hers. 'You . . . do. . . not. . . know. . . what. . . has. . . happened!' she spoke slowly, her tongue striking her front gum, the jaw moving stiffly, as though partly paralysed. She loosed her left hand and held up the curved work-worn fingers before her daughter-in-law's face. 'Was it not told me . . . the night he was born . . . here . . . at this spot . . . that he would do great things . . . great things . . . for his land and his people?' She bent forward till her lips almost touched the other's. 'Three . . . bullet . . . wounds . . . and four . . . bayonet . . . stabs!' She raised her left hand high in the air. 'Three . . . bullet . . . wounds . . . and four . . . bayonet . . . stabs! . . Is it given to many to die so for their land and their people!'

The younger woman gazed into her eyes, her own growing larger and larger. She let the old woman lead her by the arm in silence into the house.

The field cornet's son was gone, feeling there was nothing more to be done; and the Kaffir woman went back with her baby to her hut beyond the kraals. All day the house was very silent. The Kaffir woman wondered that no smoke rose from the farmhouse chimney, and that she was not called to churn, or wash the pots. At three o'clock she went down to the house. As she passed the grated window of the round out-house she saw the buckets of milk still standing unsifted on the floor as they had been set down at breakfast time, and under the great soap-pot beside the wood pile the fire had died out. She went round to the front of the house and saw the door and window shutters still closed, as though her mistresses were still sleeping. So she rebuilt the fire under the soap-pot and went back to her hut.

It was four o'clock when the grandmother came out from the dark inner room where she and her daughter-in-law had been lying down; she opened the top of the front door, and lit the fire with twigs, and set the large black kettle over it. When it boiled she made coffee, and poured out two cups and set them on the table with a plate of biscuits, and then called her daughter-in-law from the inner room.

The two women sat down one on each side of the table, with their coffee cups before them, and the biscuits between them, but for a time they said nothing, but sat silent, looking through the open door at the shadow of the house and the afternoon sunshine beyond it. At last the older woman motioned that the younger should drink her coffee. She took a little, and then folding her arms on the table rested her head on them, and sat motionless as if asleep.

The older woman broke up a biscuit into her own cup, and stirred it round and round; and then, without tasting, sat gazing out into the afternoon's sunshine till it grew cold beside her.

It was five, and the heat was quickly dying; the glorious golden colouring of the later afternoon was creeping over everything when she rose from her chair. She moved to the door and took from behind it two white calico bags hanging there, and from nails on the wall she took down two large brown cotton kappies. She walked round the table and laid her hand gently on her daughter-in-law's arm. The younger woman raised her head slowly and looked up into her mother-in-law's face; and then, suddenly, she knew that her mother-in-law was an old, old, woman. The little shrivelled face that looked down at her was hardly larger than a child's, the eyelids were half closed and the lips worked at the corners and the bones cut out through the skin in the temples.

'I am going out to sow – the ground will be getting too dry tomorrow; will you come with me?' she said gently.

The younger woman made a movement with her hand, as though she said, 'What is the use?' and redropped her hand on the table.

'It may go on for long, our burghers must have food,' the old woman said gently.

The younger woman looked into her face, then she rose slowly and taking one of the brown kappies from her hand, put it on, and hung one of the bags over her left arm; the old woman did the same and together they passed out of the door. As the older woman stepped down the younger caught her and saved her from falling.

'Take my arm, mother,' she said.

But the old woman drew her shoulders up. 'I only stumbled a little!' she said quickly. 'That step has been always too high'; but before she reached the plank over the sloot the shoulders had drooped again, and the neck fallen forward.

The mould in the lands was black and soft; it lay in long ridges, as it had been ploughed up a week before, but the last night's rain had softened it and made it moist and ready for putting in the seed.

The bags which the women carried on their arms were full of the seed of pumpkins and mealies. They began to walk up the lands, keeping parallel with the low hedge of dried bushes that ran up along the side of the sloot almost up to the top of the ridge. At every few paces they stopped and bent down to press into the earth, now one and then the other kind of seed from their bags. Slowly they walked up and down till they reached the top of the land almost on the horizon line; and then they turned, and walked down, sowing as they went. When they had reached the bottom of the land before the farmhouse it was almost sunset, and their bags were nearly empty; but they turned to go up once more. The light of the setting sun cast long, gaunt shadows from their figures across the ploughed land, over the low hedge and the sloot, into the bare veld beyond; shadows that grew longer and longer as they passed slowly on pressing in the seeds . . . The seeds. . ! that were to lie in the dank, dark, earth, and rot there, seemingly, to die, till their outer covering had split and fallen from them . . . and then, when the rains had fallen, and the sun had shone, to come up above the earth again, and high in the clear air to lift their feathery plumes and hang out their pointed leaves and silken tassels! To cover the ground with a mantle of green and gold through which sunlight quivered, over which the insects hung by thousands, carrying yellow pollen on their legs and wings and making the air alive with their hum and stir, while grain and fruit ripened surely . . . for the next season's harvest!

When the sun had set, the two women with their empty bags turned and walked silently home in the dark to the farmhouse.

Nineteen Hundred and One

Near one of the camps in the northern Transvaal are the graves of two women. The older one died first, on the twenty-third of the month, from hunger and want; the younger woman tended her with ceaseless care and devotion till the end. A week later when the British superintendent came round to inspect the tents, she was found lying on her blanket on the mud floor dead, with the rations of bread and meat she had got four days before untouched on a box beside her. Whether she died of disease, or from inability to eat the food, no one could say. Some who had seen her said she hardly seemed to care to live after the old woman died; they buried them side by side.

There is no stone and no name upon either grave to say who lies there . . . our unknown . . . our unnamed . . . our forgotten dead.

In the Year Nineteen Hundred and Four

If you look for the little farmhouse among the ridges you will not find it there today.

The English soldiers burnt it down. You can only see where the farmhouse once stood, because the stramonia and weeds grow high and very strong there; and where the ploughed lands were you can only tell, because the veld never grows quite the same on land that has once been ploughed. Only a brown patch among the long grass on the ridge shows where the kraals and huts once were.

In a country house in the north of England the owner has upon his wall an old flintlock gun. He takes it down to show his friends. It is a small thing he picked up in the war in South Africa, he says. It must be at least eighty years old and is very valuable. He shows how curiously it is constructed; he says it must have been kept in such perfect repair by continual polishing for the steel shines as if it were silver. He does not tell that he took it from the wall of the little mud house before he burnt it down.

It was the grandfather's gun, which the women had kept polished on the wall.

In a London drawing-room the descendant of a long line of titled forefathers entertains her guests. It is a fair room, and all that money can buy to make life soft and beautiful is there.

On the carpet stands a little dark wooden stofie. When one of her guests notices it, she says it is a small curiosity which her son brought home to her from South Africa when he was out in the war there; and how good it was of him to think of her when he was away in the back country. And when they ask what it is, she says it is a thing Boer women have as a foot-stool and to keep their feet warm; and she shows the hole at the side where they put the coals in, and the little holes at the top where the heat comes out.

And the other woman puts her foot out and rests it on the stofie just to try how it feels, and drawls 'How f-u-n-n-y!'

It is grandmother's stofie, that the child used to sit on.

The wagon chest was found and broken open just before the thatch caught fire, by three private soldiers, and they divided the money between them; one spent his share in drink, another had his stolen from him, but the third sent his home to England to a girl in the East End of London. With part of it she bought a gold brooch and earrings, and the rest she saved to buy a silk wedding-dress when he came home.

A syndicate of Jews in Johannesburg and London

have bought the farm. They purchased it from the English government, because they think to find gold on it. They have purchased it and paid for it ... but they do not possess it.

Only the men who lie in their quiet graves upon the hillside, who lived on it, and loved it, possess it; and the piles of stones above them, from among the long waving grasses, keep watch over the land.

(*Hanover, Cape Colony, 1905*)

Olive Schreiner

THE STORY OF AN AFRICAN FARM

The Story of an African Farm was first published in 1883, under the pseudonym Ralph Iron. Only later did it transpire that the author was actually a woman – Olive Schreiner. When the book first appeared it was received with mixed feelings by its Victorian readers, some of whom were shocked by the 'morality' of the author, and felt that it would have been better if the book had never been published. Schreiner's perseverance paid off, and today the novel, set on a farm in the Karoo, is considered important for South African literature, as the beginning of a national literary tradition. This new paperbook edition is introduced by Cherry Clayton.

281 pages, a paperbook